A Life That Satisfies:
Free Your Self By Choice, Commitment, & Cooperation

Will Crichton PhD

Edited by Carl Semmelroth PhD

Voluntary Living Press
Kalamazoo Michigan

Published by Voluntary Living Press

Library of Congress Control Number: 2011944878

For information from publisher:
Voluntary Living Press
3219 Lorraine
Kalamazoo, MI 49008
voluntarylivingpress@gmail.com

ISBN: 0-9826232-1-6
ISBN-13: 978-0-9826232-1-3

CONTENTS

1 What Are You?

You have a body, desires, fears, anger, emotions, likes, dislikes sympathies, and aversions. Are these you?

You have an occupation, a certain status in society, a certain image that you present to those who know you. You may have several images. Are these you?

You also have beliefs, attitudes, and preoccupations.

You are, in a way, all these things. And we could go on to mention your skills, the language you speak, the social customs you share, the moral values you share and practice. These are also, in a way, part of you.

But where in all this is your power of choice? All of these things influence your choices. But do they choose? Does your body choose? To think in this way would be to pretend that things are merely happening to you. You control your body, not the other way around.

Do your desires make you choose? You may desire to eat a piece of cake but refrain from doing so for the sake of your health. Your power of choice can override your desire. Do your fears make you choose? You may act in spite of fear. Your power of choice can override your fear.

You are an agent of choice:

Do your beliefs make you choose? You can question your beliefs and change them. Is it not rather that you choose to believe instead of your beliefs making you choose?

You are an agent of choice; this much is clear. You may doubt whether you are really any of the things mentioned above, but it is beyond doubt that, whatever else you are, you are an agent of choice.

Starting with this simple insight, there is a way of thinking about yourself that will allow your power of choice to stand out clearly. It will liberate your power of choice.

This way of thinking was discovered, or perhaps we should say invented, by The Buddha in ancient India. Most of the first few chapters of this book is based on a central point of his teaching, expressed here in a way more suitable to modern Western minds, and removed from its original religious and philosophical context. Fear not, I am not asking you to become a Buddhist, nor am I a Buddhist. You do not have to be a Buddhist to make use of the wisdom of The Buddha, any more than you have to be a Jew to make use of the wisdom of the Hebrew prophets, or a Christian to make use of the wisdom of Christ.

2 Perspective on Desire

Let us consider a common predicament. You are overweight. The cause of your excess weight is that you eat too much, especially of fattening foods such as sweet desserts. To an unsympathetic bystander the solution is very simple - eat less, and eat a better balanced diet. But to you it is not simple at all. You cannot control your eating.

Most of the programs for bringing your diet under control involve some form or other of playing tricks on yourself. You set up a special discipline that you follow strictly, and you are ashamed to depart from it. Perhaps it involves special incentives and rewards here and there. It may involve joining a society or group and so adding an element of moral support while strengthening the factor of shame if you deviate from the program. Perhaps it involves paying a sizeable fee for the program, making you reluctant to deviate and so waste your money.

To some readers this list will be painfully familiar. All these devices involve setting up some external influence, which with the help of an "effort of will", is supposed to trick you into eating a more suitable diet. It often works.

But let us say you bring your weight down to the desired level; what then? Are you going to continue your Spartan program for the rest of your life? A depressing prospect! Or are you going to lapse back into your old habits and go through the cycle all over again? A discouraging prospect.

Let us consider something different, something more fundamental.

You are an agent of choice. You have certain desires for food that you have hitherto considered uncontrollable. In other words, you have thought of your desire as something that determined your choice.

You, an agent of choice, are not the same thing as your objects of concern:

Now begin thinking in a different way. Your desire is not what chooses. You, the agent of choice, are not the same as you, the craver of food. Think of these as two separate thin

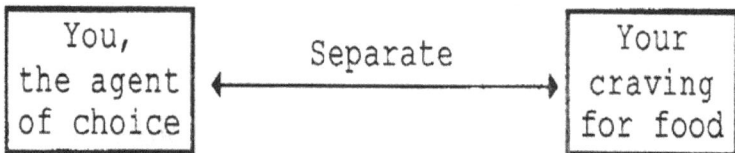

You, the agent of choice	Separate	Your craving for food

Think of you, the agent of choice, as the real or central you. This is reasonable enough, is it not? Your craving for food then becomes one of the things this central you has to live

4

with. It becomes an object, disconnected from your choices, something to be taken into account along with other things when you choose to eat or not eat this or that food. It is just one among your objects of concern.

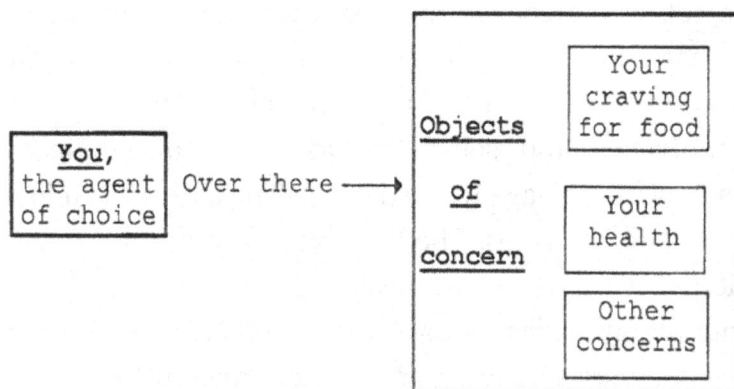

```
┌──────────────────────────────────────┐
│                         ┌──────────┐  │
│                         │  Your    │  │
│                Objects  │ craving  │  │
│                         │ for food │  │
│  ┌───────────┐          └──────────┘  │
│  │   You,    │                        │
│  │ the agent │ Over there ──→   of    │
│  │ of choice │          ┌──────────┐  │
│  └───────────┘          │  Your    │  │
│                         │ health   │  │
│                concern  └──────────┘  │
│                         ┌──────────┐  │
│                         │  Other   │  │
│                         │ concerns │  │
│                         └──────────┘  │
└──────────────────────────────────────┘
```

The idea is simple, but you need to practice in order to put it into practice. Say to yourself, "Here am I, the agent of choice. Over there is my desire for food. It is not part of me, the agent of choice. It is like the bruise on my hand that I can put medicine on or simply ignore. In the same way, I can either eat or not eat, regardless of my desire. My desire may be an irritant, but it need not determine my choice."

You can dispel the illusion that desire determines your choices:

And of course, this is true. It must be true, since it is a plain fact that people do not always indulge their desires. The Buddha's method is essentially a trick of thought, but it does not depend on illusion. Rather, it depends on a basic insight about choice and helps you to acquire that same insight. Far from cultivating an illusion, it enables you to dispel an illusion - the illusion that your desire determines your choice.

Desire does not determine your choice. If it seems to, it is because you, the agent of choice, are taking orders from your desire, rather than being the master in your own house.

It has often been thought that The Buddha taught the eradication of desire. This is not true at all. He criticized both self-indulgence and self-denial as forms of bondage. The hedonist is in bondage to his desires. The ascetic is in bondage to his ascetic doctrines. The Buddha referred to his method as a middle way. It is the way of accurate thinking and appropriate attitudes and actions. At its basis is the principle of dispassionate judgment and choice. And so far as desire is concerned, this depends on thinking of your desires as objects, different from yourself, the agent of choice. It is the method of the detached agent of choice, though this was not quite The Buddha's own way of putting it.

The idea is not to deny yourself, but simply to do the sensible thing. There are healthy desires and unhealthy desires. The idea is to indulge the healthy ones and not the unhealthy ones. There are timely and untimely desires. The idea is to indulge the timely ones and not the untimely ones. You can do it because you, the agent of choice, are in fact detachable from your desires.

Think of this method of detachment as a way of making self-control easy. The usual way of thinking about the dynamics of choice is to think of a contest of forces. There are various desires, fears, emotions, ambitions, and so forth, each pushing you in its own direction. Among these forces is supposed to be a special one called "will-power". When you are trying to overcome an unhealthy desire, the thought is that you make an effort of will, and if you have a strong enough will, you succeed in pushing the desire aside, but if the desire, is stronger you give in and indulge it.

You can choose to do what you value as the right thing to do:

But this is not what happens. The struggle is not between your will and your desire. The struggle is a state of indecisiveness in which you are vacillating between self-indulgence and what you know to be the right course. This appears as a contest between opposing forces because you are thinking of your desire as a force moving you to choose. In order to make this story come out right you label your knowledge of what you ought to do as your "will". As though to indulge your desire would not be an act of will on your part but more like being blown over by the wind. But if you think of your desire, not as a force, but as one among many things to be taken into account, your indecisiveness will no longer appear to be a contest of opposing forces, but simply a state of indecisiveness.

You are then free to do what seems best. Your power of choice has been released from the chains of an illusory dependence. This makes self-control easy, because it is then clear that you, the agent of choice, are the master, while, you, the desires, emotions, etc., are the organism to be managed and kept in order.

Desire for food is only one of many desires, and desire is only one of many passions. The method of detachment applies in the same way to fear, anger, likes, dislikes, excitement, boredom, compassion, envy, jealousy, - the whole array of attractions, aversions, and emotions.

There are two mistaken ways of thinking about these attractions, aversions, and emotions. One is to think of these as your essential vital forces, so that indulging them seems to be the essence of a satisfying life; this leads to discontentment and chaos.

The other mistaken way is to think of these as defects of nature, as irrational interferences with orderly and virtuous living, to be subdued and eliminated if possible; this leads to arbitrariness, to a drab life of pointless dogma and discipline.

Desires, aversions, and emotions are sources of information, not vital forces or defects:

The third way, the way of detachment, is to treat your passions as sources of information. They tell you the state you are in. If properly trained, they tell you what you will enjoy and what you will not enjoy, what will be healthy and what unhealthy. As sources of information, they are objects to be considered, not identified with you the agent of choice, but with you the organism to be managed. They also become objects to be enjoyed, when this is appropriate, and it is you enjoying them, not them driving you.

3 The Detached Agent of Choice

Now let us consider the scope of this method of detachment. The idea is to single out this one aspect of yourself – yourself as agent of choice – and think of *everything else* as an object, not something that determines your choice but something to be considered while you determine your choice.

These other things include all those things you already think of as objects, such as houses and trees. We need not dwell on these.

Where the method makes a difference is with regard to those things you are apt to think of as putting pressure on you to do this or that. And they are many.

We may classify them under five headings.

1. Inclinations
2. Sensations, feelings, and emotions
3. Other aspects of "self"
4. Social conventions and expectations
5. Physical things associated with you

Let us say you have certain ambitions, You may be "driven" by your ambition. Your friends may see what you do not see, that your pursuit of this ambition is out of proportion to its importance. Now, if you would cultivate the point of view of the detached agent of choice, you could see the matter with the same objectivity as do your friends.

Point of view of your detached agent of choice is objective:

What is objectivity? It is considering matters as objects rather than as "self" or as anti-"self". To use psychologists' language, it is considering matters in a non-ego-involved way. It is detaching them from that aspect of self which is the agent of choice.

How to view your ambition objectively:

Seeing your ambition as an object of concern rather than as something driving you does not mean abandoning it. Not at all. It means being able to see it in perspective along with other matters of concern. In some cases, it might lead you to pursue your ambition more vigorously rather than less. It might enable you to see its importance more clearly.

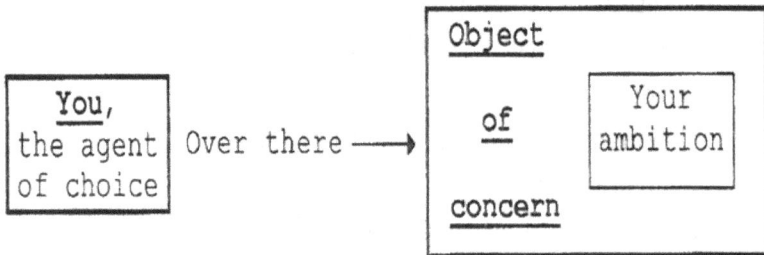

```
 _____                        _____
|  You,          |                      | Object                           |
| the agent      | Over there ──▶       |           _____       |
| of choice      |                      |  of      | Your           |     |
|_____|                      |          | ambition       |     |
                                        |          |_____|     |
                                        | concern                         |
                                        |_____|
```

View your body objectively:

Let us say you have a beautiful body. Some people have a compulsive concern with their bodily appearance. Such a compulsion does not always result in a more attractive appearance. Often it results in exaggerated grooming which detracts from appearance. To rid yourself of such a compulsion, cultivate the point of view of the detached agent of choice. This may seem very difficult with regard to your body, since we are accustomed to think of ourselves as one and the same as our bodies.

But practice this exercise: think: here am I, the agent of choice; down there is my body. In other words, imagine yourself rising above your body and looking down on it.

Or, you may try another exercise. Look at you hand. Think: this hand is not part of me, the agent of choice, but is one of the things I am concerned about, in the same way as I am concerned about my house or my shoes.

When you have become accustomed to this thought, do the same with your feet, then your legs, your torso, your arms, and finally, your head. Now, is it so unnatural to think of your body as an object of concern rather than something making you do things?

When you do this you will, begin to look at your body with the same objectivity that other people have about it. Is it as important as you thought it was? Is it perhaps more important than you thought it was? Is it important in different ways and for different reasons than you thought? These questions, to which your mind was closed, may now occur to you.

```
┌──────────────┐          ┌─────────────────────────────┐
│  You,        │          │ Object                      │
│  the agent   │ Over there ──▶│   of    │  Your        │
│  of choice   │          │         │  body        │
└──────────────┘          │ concern                     │
                          └─────────────────────────────┘
```

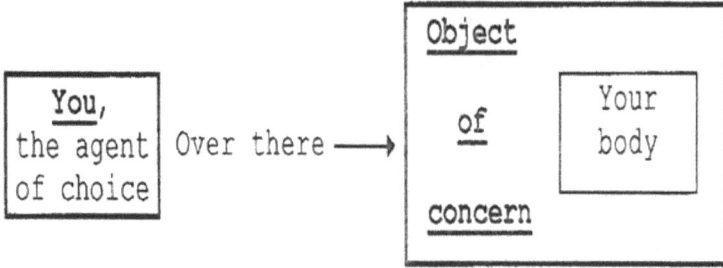

How to view your community status objectively:

You have a certain status in the community. You have an important job, or you are a pillar of the church, for example. Perhaps you think of yourself as locked into this status or role, so that you must act as is expected of you. This way of thinking is not most conducive to doing your job most effectively or to making your best contribution to your church. It deprives you of your objectivity about those very functions you are so concerned to perform.

Think of your status or role as something "out there", separate from you, the agent of choice. It is one of your objects of concern, not something making you do things.

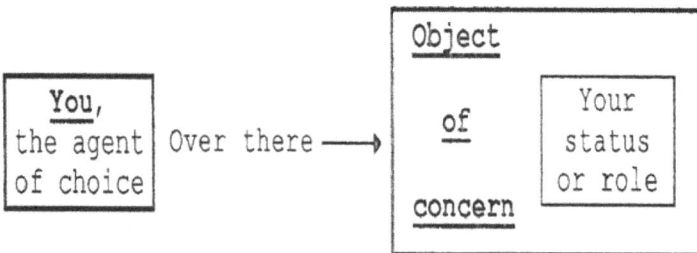

```
┌──────────────┐          ┌─────────────────────────────┐
│  You,        │          │ Object                      │
│  the agent   │ Over there ──▶│   of    │  Your status │
│  of choice   │          │         │  or role     │
└──────────────┘          │ concern                     │
                          └─────────────────────────────┘
```

With this point of view, you can see your status more clearly for what it is. Perhaps you have been devoting too much of your time and energy to it, to the neglect of your home life, and with the result that you have become stale, or dogmatic, or overbearing. Perhaps you have seen your role too much in terms of a conventional image rather than in terms of what it is meant to accomplish. These are some of the questions your mind will become open to and able to consider dispassionately if you cultivate the point of view of the detached agent of choice.

How to view your beliefs objectively:

You have certain beliefs that you have held for some time. You think of these beliefs as part of yourself – that they make you what you are. Now, this may be quite true in a way. But to think in this way without separating your power of choice from other aspects of your "self" is to exempt these beliefs from objective consideration.

But, you may say, you would not under any circumstances question their truth. So be it. But how are you to apply these beliefs as guides for living? If you exempt them from objective consideration, you put them behind a veil. How then can you properly assess what it would be to really live by them? Perhaps you are not living by them at all but only using them as a kind of banner under which you march. (The banner may say "peace" while those who march under it march to war!)

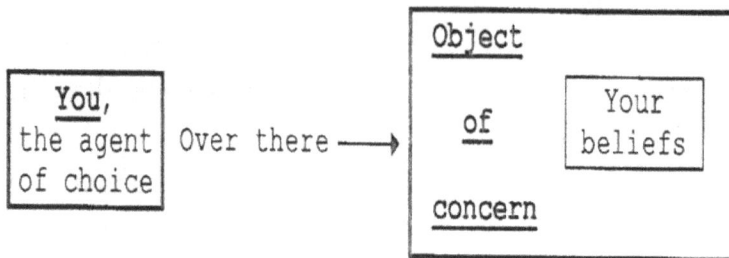

If you adopt the point of view of the detached agent of choice, you will think of your beliefs as objects, perhaps some of your principal objects of concern.

This does not mean you cast doubt on your beliefs, though of course you may. It does enable you to see them for what they are, as an impartial bystander might. Seeing them as they are, you will be able to see more clearly what it means to live by them. If you are serious about them as one who really believes, not as a hypocrite, will you not welcome such an insight?

How to view "social pressures" objectively:

These are some of the aspects of "self". What about the influence of society? We sometimes speak of "social pressures" or "the pressure to conform". You feel this as a pressure if you are being expected to do something you would rather not do, or to refrain from doing something you would rather do.

Why should you feel it as a pressure? You can either do or not do the thing in question. It is true that you have an identification with the community, and so you should have. (I will stress this later under the heading of "the threefold self".) But the feeling of social pressure comes from identifying, not only your interests, but also your power of choice with the community.

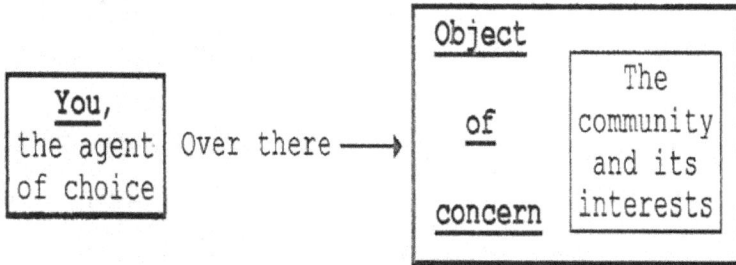

```
┌──────────────┐              ┌─────────────────────────────┐
│   You,       │              │ Object                      │
│              │ Over there → │              ┌────────────┐ │
│  the agent   │              │   of         │    The     │ │
│              │              │              │ community  │ │
│  of choice   │              │              │  and its   │ │
│              │              │ concern      │ interests  │ │
└──────────────┘              │              └────────────┘ │
                              └─────────────────────────────┘
```

Your interests should be identified with the community (or with various communities). But to identify your power of choice with the community is to give up your initiative as a member of that community. This means that your judgment as to how to contribute to the community is impaired. Your objectivity is limited, and so, therefore, is your effectiveness.

If you adopt the point of view of the detached agent of choice, these things come into perspective. You can then view your shared interests with the community objectively and also consider objectively how these interests might best be served. Thus you become a full contributor to the community. What you will then feel is not social pressure but social responsibility.

Let us list a number of the things that are not to be confused with your power of choice. You should practice applying the point of view of the detached agent of choice to each of these, and to anything else that might be of importance to you but which is not in fact the same as your power of choice.

- **Inclinations** – Desire, Aversion, Fear, Anger

- **Feelings** – Joy, Sadness, Emotions, Sympathy, Dislike, Pain, Sensation
- **"Self"** – Body, Skills, Strengths, Weaknesses, Thoughts, Beliefs, Interests, Aspirations, Reputation, Status, Role
- **Social Pressures** – Custom, Morality, Values, Doctrines, Language, Fashions, Fads, Duties, Obligations
- **Things** – Property, Possessions, Environment

How to view doctrines usefully:

To round off the chapter, let us consider doctrines. People often attach themselves to certain doctrines or to the authors of those doctrines or to the words in which those doctrines are expressed. They identify themselves as Christians, Jews, Moslems, or something else and invest the words of their great teachers with a privileged aura of wisdom.

Now, I am not suggesting that you should stop being a Christian or whatever you are. But listen to a parable told by The Buddha (which I will paraphrase from Walpola Rahula's *What The Buddha Taught*).

He told of a man who had great need to cross a river because of dangers besetting him on the side where he was. Having no means of crossing, he set about collecting pieces of wood and managed to put together a raft with which, after much effort, he reached the other shore. He then said to himself, "This raft has done me great service for which I should be eternally grateful. Therefore I will fasten it on my back and carry it for the rest of my journey, as a mark of my gratitude to it."

"Now," asked The Buddha of his pupils, "was that the proper way to deal with the raft?"

"No," they replied, "he should have left it on the bank in case some other traveler might find it useful."

"Just so," answered The Buddha, "and it is the same with my teachings. They should not be carried about as a burden but treated as something useful, and passed on to others in that spirit."

In other words, adopt the point of view of the detached agent of choice to doctrines, even to those that tell of the detached agent of choice. Only then will you be able to see them in their true light and derive their full benefit in practice. Only then can you be like "the house built on a rock" in a parable told by another great teacher. The solid foundation of understanding, he meant, is found in the "doing", not the "hearing".

4 The Essential Self

Liberating your power of choice by the method of detachment may possibly leave you with the impression that you are not really anything but an ability to choose. That you are, as Jean-Paul Sartre put it, "a nothingness in the midst of reality." You may then think that whatever you do is arbitrary and insupportable by any reasons, or that you have no genuine interests in the world.

Your self is more than an agent of choice:

But to think this way is to suppose that 'agent of choice' is the only genuine meaning of 'self'. This is to put a wrong meaning on the notion of detachment. It is like saying that because the camera is not the same as the thing being photographed, it makes no difference which way it is aimed. It's like saying that because the thing being photographed does not control the aim of the camera, it can be disregarded when aiming the camera. In fact it can, but ought not. The camera is not all of photography, nor is the agent of choice all of the self.

To treat as an object everything but your power of choice is not to regard these other things as unimportant. It is only to set them in perspective so that their importance can be judged and the best way of acting with regard to them can be decided. To bear this in mind is to be protected against the kind of nihilism described above

Nevertheless, when we consider the many connotations of 'self' and the way they shade off into social involvements and even inanimate things such as one's property, we are left with a question about the self. What is the essential self, if indeed there is any such thing?

Finding your essential self:

Let us make a threefold distinction.
- There is the world in which you exist, which includes other agents of choice.
- There is yourself as agent of choice.
- And there are your commitments.

These are all different. Your commitments are not a feature of the world in which you exist. They are rather your way of proceeding in that world.

Nor are your commitments the same as your power of choice. Rather, they are acts or products of your power of choice; they are in fact choices. They have no continuing existence except as you continue to choose in that manner.

You can apply the point of view of the detached agent of choice to your commitments. You can set your commitments "over there" as objects.

Let us say you are determined to be a good father or mother. You can think as follows: Here am I, the agent of choice; over there is the idea of my being a good parent. By thinking in this way, you are able to consider this idea objectively in relation to your circumstances and so implement it effectively.

Commitments come from you, not to you:

But there is a difference between your commitments and the things discussed in the last chapter. These other things, such as your desires, your body, your ambitions, your status, are things that come to you from the world around you or from your own development. Even your ambitions are a kind of emotion that you feel. But your commitments come from you rather than to you. When you consider your commitments as objects, you are not considering feelings or impressions or obligations, but intentions.

You are not considering the commitments you have had in the past. These take the form of your obligations, ambitions, frustrations, accomplishments. All these are things which, at the present moment, come *to* you. On the other hand, your present commitments determine what you are as you enter the future. Therefore, when you consider your commitments as objects you are considering proposals for the future, whether in the short run or the long run.

You are in the world. You cannot act independently of it. Your commitments must take the form of your projected future in this world. These are the objects that you set before yourself as agent of choice.

Why would you set them before you in this way? In order to set your course with open eyes. In order to *have* a course and not drift aimlessly. In order to be fully living, a fully active participant, not merely at odd moments but in a life which sits solidly over time, in order to live *in* time *with a quality* of eternity. In order to *be,* both in and above the world.

Commitments bring reality to choice:

You are an agent of choice. But if the agent does not act it has no content, no substance. It would then truly be a mere nothingness within reality. It is the agent in act which has being. It is by actually committing yourself to certain interests that you acquire reality. And the more your commitments both overarch and also penetrate time the fuller the reality you will have. In other words, the more you integrate the long run with the short runs the more fully you will live.

Now, not only are you in the world, but you have a past. Not only must you form your commitments in and for the real world, but you must form them on the foundation of your own inner heritage. This is the principal of "karma". What you can be next is limited by what you have been. This does not mean that you cannot rise above your past. It does mean that you must proceed from your present. It is like travelling. If you are in Toronto you may travel to New York, but you must travel from Toronto through locations between Toronto and New York. You cannot simply be in New York.

You may not like your past. You may wish to change radically. You can do so, but it is futile to attempt a sudden leap to a life for which you have no preparation. This will founder in disarray. You must find in your own inner heritage the point of departure for what you will be.

The full life is one that gathers its resources from the past and gathers the future together.

You will not find your essential self within or without. You must create it starting with commitments:

We may begin, then, to comprehend the essential self. It is not something you can find by searching within yourself, still less by searching around the world. Its resources are in the past, and its actuality is your present commitment for the future. You cannot find it. You must create it.

How are you to go about this? We are not speaking about making plans, though you will probably want to make plans. But you will also want your commitments to transcend the unpredictability of the world. You must seek the most important things. Your commitment to these will be your most fundamental commitment. This is the inner core of the essential self.

How may you seek the most important things? You need some quiet moments. You need to get beyond the immediate facts of the moment, not to some world beyond this one, but to the depths of your experience. You have perhaps never been conscious of those depths except as a hint, or an enticing (or disturbing) fantasy, or a wistful glimpse of something superior. But do not fall into the error of wishing for circumstances more pleasing than your actual ones. This leads to self-pity rather than commitment.

Again, the technique of the detached agent of choice is the key. Put yourself as agent of choice over here. Put your visions of your commitments for the future over there. Contemplate them.

Which of them would be most completely satisfying? Which of them makes the best picture? Remember, it is commitments you are contemplating, not fortunes. What may happen to you is not yours to choose. What you will be is yours to choose. It is what you are always choosing. It is what you cannot escape choosing.

5 Inner Peace

It is not enough to understand what has been said in these chapters. Intellectual understanding can be an excuse for evading practical issues. One says, "Yes, I see the point", and then does nothing to put it into practice. This is like saying, "Don't worry, I know how to wash the dishes", and then not washing them. To understand the liberation of your power of choice is not to liberate your power of choice.

I have described for a number of cases the kind of exercise you should do to cultivate the point of view of the detached agent of choice. It is up to you to actually do these exercises if you wish to achieve the result.

The result is not any sort of ecstasy or "cosmic consciousness", or the sorts of experience that people in the West have imagined to be the result of Oriental techniques of meditation. I would describe the *feeling* that comes from cultivating the point of view of the detached agent of choice as one of being clean, unencumbered, and clear-minded. It is a feeling that, when I first experienced it, was the impression of being released from a multitude of harassments. It was a feeling of wonderful peace.

Ceasing the harassment from within brings peace:

It is in fact a matter of being released from harassments. The harassments, however, are not imposed from without. Oh yes, there are external harassments, and these do not go away. The release is not an escape from the business of living. It is a release from harassments of your own making. It is a deliverance from your own confusion between your power of choice and other things. The confusion is to think of things you should, or might, take into account when choosing, as if they were making you choose.

For example, your fear of a certain situation is something you should take into account in deciding whether to enter that situation or not. Your fear is probably a sign of some inadequacy or lack of preparation on your part, and this should be considered before deciding. But if you think of your fear as something forcing you to avoid the situation, then in order to enter it you not only **have** to compensate for your inadequacy but have to overcome your fear as well. If you choose to be governed by your fear, it is the same as if you were governed by it. But if you think of your fear only as something to be taken into account, then you are free to deal, with your inadequacy.

Review all the things you are accustomed to thinking of as impelling you to do or not do this or that, or as impelling you to think in certain ways or not think in certain ways. Perform the exercise of detaching yourself as agent of choice and regarding them as objects to be taken into account. Bit by bit, perhaps suddenly, you will begin to feel a great weight of oppression falling away and leaving you, the agent, separate, free, disburdened, and clean.

Consider the things mentioned earlier under the heading of "self," such as ambition, status, reputation, abilities. And consider your cravings, your fears, your resentments, your indignations.

Imagine being released from the impelling force of all these, not in the sense that they will no longer exist, but in the sense that their "force" will no longer affect your ability to choose. They will be there like a passing picture, not like something pushing you.

Extinguish the fevered nature of ambition, status, reputation, abilities, cravings, fears, resentments, & indignations:

If this inner peace were achieved completely, so that yourself as agent of choice stood forth completely clean and unencumbered this would be what The Buddha called nirvana, or so I interpret the texts. The Sanskrit word nirvana means the extinction or going out of a flame. The encumbrances I have referred to may be compared to a burning or fever of the self. The person "burning with ambition", not merely pursuing it, the person "burning with indignation", and so on, are like patients suffering from a fever. The detached point of view cools that fever, and the experience of it is akin to that of cool water applied to a fevered brow. The flame is extinguished.

You need not think of <u>nirvana</u> in ideal terms. It is something that can be experienced whenever you achieve the detachment of your power of choice. To whatever degree and in whatever respects you attain it, to that degree and in those respects you will be enabled to think and act with cool detachment when you so choose. It will not prevent you from acting with passion, emotion, or excitement when that seems appropriate. The choice will be yours.

6 Seeing Things Clearly

When you cultivate the separation of your power of choice from other things, you become aware of the difference between them. You become aware of yourself as agent of choice. In so doing you also become sensitive to the difference between those things which are the products of your choice and those things which are not.

This distinction is already a familiar one, without any special disciplines. When you bump into the table, the table itself is not a product of your initiative at that moment, but your movement so as to bump into it is (not that you intended to bump into the table but that you moved by your own initiative). If you make a remark and someone else makes a remark in reply, your remark is a product of your initiative, but the other person's remark is not. You did not make his remark.

To become aware of the difference between those things that are products of your initiative and those things that are not is not to become aware of something previously unknown. It is only to sharpen that awareness. It is to notice things that previously went unnoticed.

Clarify those things that are a product of your initiative and those things that are not:

For example, when someone else responds to your remark with another remark, it is true that you set up the circumstances in which he made his remark. But you did not initiate his remark, He did. In the same way, if you respond to someone else's remark with another remark, say an angry retort, he did not initiate your remark. He only set up the circumstances in which *you* initiated it. He did not make you angry, except in the sense that you were prepared to be angry under certain circumstances, and he set up those circumstances.

As a start towards seeing things more clearly, you may think of reality as being made up of yourself as agent of choice, other agents of choice, and still other things that are not agents of choice. Among these other things are some which exist only as choices on your part, such as your opinions, your attitudes, your ways of thinking about things, your interpretations of what passes through your awareness.

Then there are other things that are not choices on your part, such as the choices of others and things that do not seem to be choices at all and, in any case, are not human choices, such as stones, water, and trees.

Now, if you are to see things more clearly, it must be by clarifying your awareness.

```
┌─────────────┐
│   You,      │            ┌──────────┐
│ as agent    │──────────▶ │ Choices  │
│ of choice   │            └──────────┘
└─────────────┘
                                        ┌──────────┐
                                        │  Other   │
                                        │  things  │
                                        └──────────┘
┌─────────────┐
│   Other     │            ┌──────────┐
│  agents     │──────────▶ │ Choices  │
│ of choice   │            └──────────┘
└─────────────┘
```

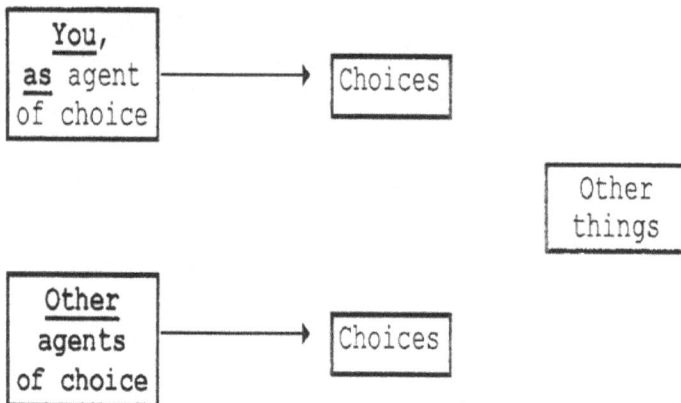

When you have an awareness, you are doing something. You may be directing your eyes in a certain *way,* or holding your hand against something so as to feel its texture or vibration. There are many things of this sort you may be doing. But at the very least you are paying attention to something that is happening. This that you are doing, whatever it is, is your choice. It sets up the situation in which something that is happening happens *to you*. The result is an awareness.

Then there is a second factor in your awareness, something that is not your choice. This is what we might call *the passing show*. It is that part of your awareness that happens to you.

The "passing show" happens to you. Your interpretation of it is something you do:

Finally, there is normally a third element in your awareness. This is the interpretation you attach to the passing show. For example, you think, "there goes a brass band', or "there is someone at the door", or "the motor has stopped running." This third element, like the first, is something you do. It is your choice to put that interpretation on the passing show.

The first element, what you do to precipitate the awareness, being your choice, is immediate to you. You can become aware of it. You can learn to control it. It is susceptible to the point of view of the detached power of choice.

The passing show is also immediate to you, not as something you can control, but as something you can be sure is there.

This passing show is not the brass band or someone at the door or the motor stopping. It is what has happened to you. But a brass band is more than that. It has a past and a future; it has a purpose; it has a place in the social structure; it has a meaning within the structure of your values, preferences, and ideas. These things are not in the passing show as such. They are how you interpret the passing show.

You are taking the passing show as a sign of things that are immediate to you.

The passing show is your evidence for the existence at that time and place of the brass band. The passing show itself is not susceptible of doubt or uncertainty. It is immediate to you. The brass band, with its past and future, its role in society, and its significance to you, is susceptible of doubt. It is possible that you are putting a mistaken construction on the passing show.

It may seem rather ridiculous to raise such doubts, but in fact, mistakes of interpretation are common. You may think someone is at the door when in fact the sound was made by someone in the house.

There are, then, these three elements of awareness:

- Your choice which brings the awareness to you, or you to it
- The passing show which that choice admits into your awareness
- What you take to be there as evidenced by the passing show.

The first two of these are immediate to you and not susceptible of doubt. The third is your conjecture. It is in fact another choice on your part, though it is intended to correspond to actualities that are not your choice.

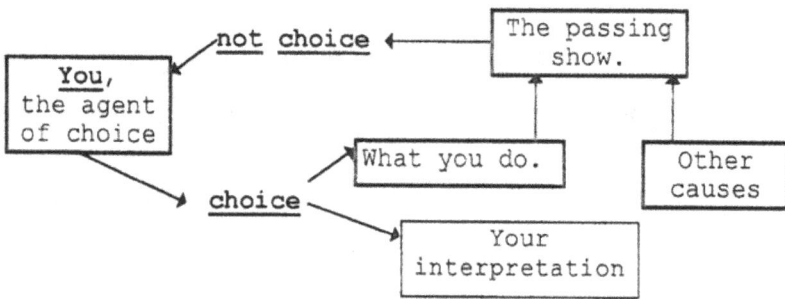

If you learn to see these aspects of your awareness for what they are, you will begin to experience clarity of perception. At one point in my own study of the Buddhist writings, it seemed as though a veil had been removed from my sight and was for the first time seeing things as they really were. The veil was the fabric of interpretations with which I constructed my experience. For, experience is much more than awareness.

The effect is the same as with the other uses of the method of detachment. But in this case, what is crucial is that you notice the difference between what is your choice and what is not your choice. This enables you to see clearly what you have chosen and what has happened to you that is not of your choosing - the passing show. It is these things that you come to see as they are, for these are the things that are immediate to you. The things that are not immediate to you, such as the brass band, are not seen as they are, but what you do see clearly is that you do not see them as they are, and that you must judge them as well as you can in the tight of the evidence.

The evidence, that is, the original and primary evidence on which you must depend, is the passing show in the context of what you have done to precipitate it, and against the background of your memory and the understanding you already have of reality. When these things are seen clearly, you can begin to form your conceptions of reality intelligently, objectively, with clarity of perception.

The removal of the veil is the removal of the confusion between the passing show and your interpretation of it. For, we are accustomed to suppose that our interpretations are what we see and feet. Because of this confusion we think we are sure of what is realty conjecture. And because we have not become aware of the passing show for what it is, we sense nothing sharply. What we call being sure is not really being sure; we have never experienced being really sure.

When you begin to see these things clearly, you will be sure of less, but you will discover what it is to be really sure. The passing show will stand out sharply, and you will discover that there is more to it than you might have guessed.

7 The Advantage and the Risk

To know what choices are open to you is a great advantage. If you approach a decision with an inaccurate sense of your possible choices, you are apt to make either of two mistakes. On the one hand, you may choose an option that seems the best, when in fact there is another much better one that never occurred to you as being within your choice. On the other hand, you may attempt to choose an option that is in fact not an option. It is not something you can actually do.

There is also a risk involved in this kind of liberation. Many people are protected against committing evil deeds by the kind of conscience that makes them think they could not do those things ("I just couldn't do a thing like that!")

Adopting the point of view of the detached agent of choice makes you aware of the difference between not being *able* to do something and not being *willing* to do it. Many of the deeds of which we say "I just couldn't do that" are deeds we *could* in fact do but *would* not do.

The advantage of thinking you could not do certain things is that this protects you against any temptation to do them. When you realize you *could* do them, your mind may then be open to the option of doing them.

Liberation of choice can be dangerous without an understanding of why some choices are foolish:

Therefore, the liberation of your power of choice may be a dangerous thing all by itself. It needs to be supplemented by a solid understanding of why certain kinds of choices are foolish, even though they may be superficially attractive. This is the theme of the following chapters. This understanding combined with the liberation of your power of choice provides a more secure and far-reaching protection against wrong and foolish deeds than any other kind of conscience ever could.

8 Present and Future

When you act, you act not only *for* the present moment but also for the future. Whether you intend it this way or not, it is so. Whatever you do has effects reaching into the future.

The future can be no more or less important than the present:

There are two extreme points of view as to one's concern about the present and the future. Some people are so anxious about a future some years away that they see the present moment only as a time of preparation for that future. Others see life as an adventure of the moment; they trust to luck for the day after tomorrow and assume little responsibility for their fellows, though they may be very generous within the confines of the present moment.

To those of the first kind, those who have no time for present indulgence, I put these questions:

- In what way is the future different from the present, that the present should be merely the servant of the future?
- You think of yourself as being practical; is it practical to do things for the sake of other things and never to do anything for its own sake?
- Is it practical to sow and cultivate and never to reap a harvest?
- Will you be more capable of taking satisfaction in life at some future time if you are not capable of it now? Or if you are capable of it now, why do you allot nothing to present enjoyment?

To those of the other persuasion, the adventurers of the present moment, I put these questions:

- What is this "present moment" which occupies you to the exclusion of what comes after?
- Does the present last for a period of one second? Is it a period of one hour? Of one day?
- Such a person will probably reply that it depends on what the current enjoyment is; if a party is being planned for tomorrow night, naturally it takes some preparation. Aren't you preparing for the future?
- This present in which you live is not a mere passing moment. It extends as far into the future as your current interest dictates. Why then is your interest limited to such short spans of time? Why are you content with such meager satisfactions?

By raising these questions about the two extreme points of view, we begin to see that the present and the future are not so distinct as we may be accustomed to suppose. Clocks and the science of physics have given us an artificial and misleading notion of the present. In human terms, the present is not a "point" along a mathematical scale. It is a span of events and opportunities determined by your concerns.

Our experiences of the present are not points in clock time:

There are in fact many presents with varying extensions into the past and future. If your concern is with swatting a fly, the present may be a period of a few seconds, extending from the appearance of the fly to the time of its downfall. If your concern is with preparing dinner, the present may be a period of a few hours extending from the time you begin preparations to the time when people rise from the table. If your concern is with raising your children, the present may be a period extending from the time of their birth to the tine when they become adults.

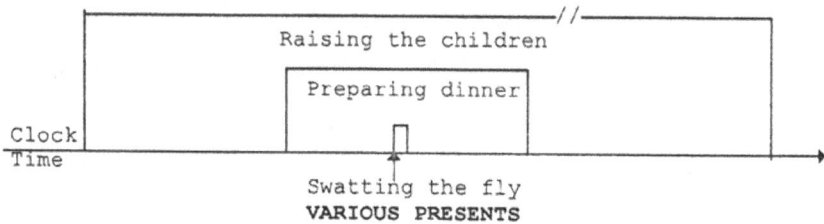

Raising the children

Preparing dinner

Clock Time

Swatting the fly

VARIOUS PRESENTS

The living present is determined by one's commitments:

"The living present" is a phrase that focuses our attention on the vividness of action and awareness. Its association with a fleeting moment of time as measured by the clock is due to a mistaken conception of experience as something happening *to* you. But what happens *to* you is only one component of experience. What you do is the more prominent component of your experience of the present. And what you do is the exercising of your commitments. The true living present is the present determined by your commitments.

Since your commitments may cover many time spans, so may there be many living presents. The richness of your life may be measured by the variety of "presents" which are truly living presents.

If you are living for today *and* for this year *and* for a twenty year period *and* for your lifetime, your life is richer than if you are only occupied with one or two of these. Nor need your present be limited to your own lifetime. Your life will be the richer for a concern with generations yet unborn, and generations past.

And beyond all these, in the fully rich life, is the timeless present which depends on a concern, not with doing, but with being. This is the being of the essential self, which I spoke of earlier. It is this timeless present which unites all the others, which gives to living in time a quality of eternity.

9 Continuity and Consistency

Your concerns: what are they? What are they made of? Let us say you have a house. It is one of your concerns. This means it is a matter of some serious interest to you. You see it as playing some part in your future affairs. In other words, you have some intentions regarding the house. You intend to live in it. You intend to entertain in it. You intend to keep it in repair. Without any such intentions you would not be concerned about the house (in the case of a stranger's house, in which you have no "direct concern", your concern, if you have any, will take the form of sympathy with the intentions of those directly involved).

Your concern has two components: some feature of reality (the house), and your intentions with regard to it.

Your concerns govern the time structure of your life – the various time spans which are your "living presents". This means that your various "living presents" are determined by the people and things on which your intentions focus, and your intentions concerning them.

Consider the significance of this when things go wrong. You have invested in a house and have pinned many of your hopes on it. Then, at some time that house is destroyed by fire. The impression this produces on you is one of your world falling apart. It is the same if someone you love suddenly and prematurely dies.

The reason your world falls apart is that the object of your intentions has been suddenly removed and you are left, in an important sense, without a future. It is the break in the continuity of your intentions which constitutes the falling apart of your world. It is a rupture of the essential self.

It is not *the* world but only *your* world that has fallen apart, not the world that enables you to live physically, but the world that you were depending on to live psychically or spiritually.

The sense of your world falling apart is not due to the prospect of hardship, but to the sudden inapplicability of your major intentions.

Let us say that your child is suddenly killed in the full bloom of youth. Now, in most cases the loss of a child is not an economic loss. In our present economic system, a child is not thought of as an essential economic asset. In crudely economic terms, the loss of a child means "one less mouth to feed". From that point of view you are better able to carry on than before. Yet, your world has fallen apart. Why? Because the object of your cherished plans has disappeared. It is the sudden inapplicability of your intentions that leaves you at a loss.

(Please note: This is not the same as your sense of injustice that someone full of vitality and hope should be snuffed out. This feeling is one you may have for someone less close to you. *Your* world need not fall apart because of this.)

On the other side of the coin, sudden hardships sometimes have the effect of putting your world together rather than making it fall apart. A marriage or a friendship may be saved from boredom and apathy by the sudden necessity of weathering a storm together. In these cases, the sudden hardship provides the occasion for intentions that had been missing, intentions that are the substance of a meaningful life - commitments.

But intentions are not the whole story, and you have perhaps been thinking of the saying that "the road to hell is paved with good intentions". Intentions that are not carried out do not provide the substance of a meaningful life. On the contrary, they undermine it, replacing it with discouragement or cynicism.

Furthermore, it is obvious that if your intentions represent what will satisfy you, that satisfaction will not be obtained by the intentions alone, but on].y by acting on them.

Your life needs two things, then:

1. Continuity in the form of intentions that draw the time spans of your life together (in other words, a well-developed essential self)
2. Consistency in the form of following through by acting on those intentions

Let us look more deeply into the subject of consistency. To say simply that you should follow through on your intentions is to ignore the uncertainties of life, and its emergencies.

We formulate our intentions in a state of moderate ignorance and often on the basis of insufficient thought. Our ability to predict future circumstances is necessarily limited, if only because of the fact that other people's choices are involved. And as for giving sufficient thought to our decisions, this is limited by the fact that we have other things to do. The world does not stop so that we can put our lives in order. We must do so "on the run" to some degree.

Therefore, our intentions are subject to some degree of unreliability. We may be mistaken in thinking that the way we intend to live, the things we intend to do, will in fact satisfy. In addition, we may not be able to carry them through. We may have misjudged the circumstances as they appeared, and they may change unpredictably.

Therefore, sometimes it is impossible to carry out your intentions, and sometimes it is reasonable to change your mind about then.

Now, by the mere fact of changing your mind you are not being inconsistent. Changing your mind would only be inconsistent if in doing so you were violating some higher intention about which you had not changed your mind. For example, if you were intending to shampoo a rug on a particular day, it would not be inconsistent to decide not to do so after all, but it would be inconsistent to just forget about it. Changing your mind about it might be inconsistent with a higher intention if, for example, you had invited guests and intended to make your house as pretty as possible for the occasion.

This shows that consistency or inconsistency is not just a blanket characteristic of what you do, but is related to particular intentions. If one intention has been formed in order to carry out a higher one, changing your mind about the subordinate intention may be consistent with it but inconsistent with the higher intention.

It may also work the other way around, if circumstances turn out contrary to what was anticipated. You may have to change your plans in order to remain true to a higher intention. This is a common occurrence.

Circumstances may change so as to render an intention no longer applicable. For example, you intend to buy a certain house but find that it has already been sold. Obviously, consistency does not require you to carry out an intention that has become meaningless. In fact, most intentions are geared to events so that they apply only at certain times. If you intend to go to a certain concert that intention can only be carried out at the time the concert is held. Thereafter it is no longer applicable.

An intention may also apply over a considerable period of time after which it becomes inapplicable. For example, you may intend to befriend a certain person by spending a certain amount of time with him. If at some time that person moves to another part of the world or dies, that intention has no further applicability. In addition, that person's need for special attention may cease, partly as a result of your kindness. In that case, also the intention may have become inapplicable so that consistency no longer requires you to continue your attentions in the same way.

What is clearly inconsistent with a particular intention is to forget all about it even though it remains applicable and you have not changed your mind about it. Consistency depends on memory and self-discipline.

Maintaining consistency of intention means acting in accordance with it until you change it or until it has no applicability:

From these observations, you can see that consistency is not a blanket characteristic of your behaviour but is related to particular intentions and the circumstances affecting them. The general principle of consistency may be stated as follows: To be consistent with a particular intention is to act and think in accordance with it until either (1.) you rescind it or (2.) it has no further applicability.

Intentions themselves need to be consistent with each other:

It is not only important to maintain intentions consistently. Intentions themselves must be consistent. Whether your basic intentions in life are good or bad, whether they are such as to afford satisfaction or otherwise, they are of no avail unless your other intentions are at least moderately consistent with them and your actions are also consistent with them. Consistency is a universal requirement of success, whether in a wise or a foolish endeavor.

A satisfying life requires wisely chosen consistent intentions, consistently maintained:

For a satisfying life, therefore, you need consistency, and you also need a system of intentions which are wisely chosen so that their achievement is inherently satisfying. Among other things, this requires the characteristic of continuity, so that you are making full use of time, not just in a minute-by-minute sense but in the richer sense of living in many times, from the indefinitely long moments which extend beyond your lifetime to the indefinitely short ones which are the seconds and minutes. Long and short here are measured by the clock and the calendar, not by the way in which you experience these time spans or moments.

The experience of long or short times depends on your point of view, not on the clock. If you are really living in the present, that is, in your many living presents, you will experience all of these living presents as timeless, since on the one hand you are savoring the experience of them, and on the other hand you are contemplating them as laid out before you like a map. The latter is the point of view of your intentions (your essential self and the detached agent of choice) and the former is the point of view of realization.

Is it within your power to achieve this with any reliability or are you at the mercy of chance? Is it only the lucky ones who are provided with those circumstances that make such a life possible? Or is it within your initiative to turn the circumstances to your advantage?

To answer these questions we must turn our attention to the issue of the highest intentions of all, the issue of basic life policies and a supreme value, for on these the rest of the fabric hangs.

10 The Threefold Self

If we are to settle the issue of basic values and policies, we need a more complete answer to the question "What are you?" If we think you are a competitor for goods and services, we will make one sort of recommendation. If we think you are a being that needs perpetual variety of stimuli, we will make a quite different recommendation. These are just two of the many ways in which people sometimes think of themselves.

The threefold self is a way of looking at yourself in a way that is helpful for making choices:

In the first few chapters, the materials for a useful answer to the question were developed. There may be many other ways of answering it that would be equally true to the facts. There are many ways of slicing a cake. But the threefold self is a way of answering "What are you?" that is specifically adapted to questions concerning choice.

An agent of choice – The Agent Self

You are first an agent of choice. Call this aspect "the agent self."

Your basic commitments define your life's essential direction – The Essential Self:

Then you have a number of basic commitments, which define the essential direction, and style of your life. I called this aspect "the essential self."

Everything you think of as yours is part of you – The Complex Self:

But you are more than this. If someone throws a stone at your car, you say he did it to you. If someone deposits money in your bank account, you say he gave it to you. It seems then, that your car and your bank account are part of you.

Whatever you can call yours is in a way part of you. We say "my power of choice, my commitments, my body, my house, my job, my town, my friend, my enemy." Yes, your enemy is as much a part of you as your friend.

These other things in addition to the agent self and the essential self I will call the complex self. I call it complex because it is just that, as complex as your associations and involvements, It includes:

- ❏ physical things such as your body or your clothing, and in general your physical environment
- ❏ persons such as your friends
- ❏ ideas that interest you

- ❑ understandings with others, such as your position in society or your credit with the bank
- ❑ social and political entities such as your family and your nation
- ❑ and others beyond my ingenuity to enumerate.

The complex self can be thought of as externalities that are part of what we are:

In short, it includes everything that is involved in your life as something for you to take into account, exclusive of your agent self and essential self. The word "self" is not normally used in such a broad sense, but for the sake of truth it is reasonable to do so, since it is in terms of all these things that your life is lived. For a convenient description, the complex self may be thought of as made up of externalities.

Just as some of your commitments are stronger or deeper than others, so some parts of your complex self are more strongly part of you than others. The complex self dwindles off into the unfamiliar, the unknown, and the irrelevant.

A meaningful life involves all three aspects of the self. You cannot avoid your power of choice, though you may disregard it. A life without commitments is devoid of continuity and perhaps impossible, since to avoid commitments may itself require a commitment to doing so. But where there are commitments there will be some sort of complex self, since the commitments themselves involve a projection of your concerns outward.

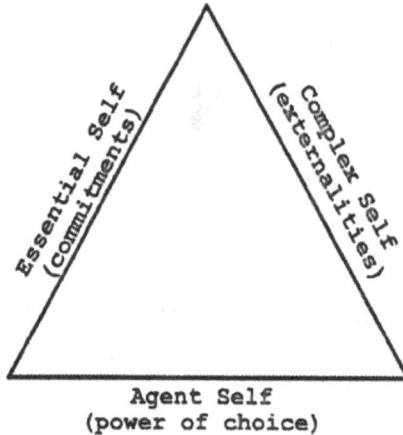

Essential Self
(commitments)

Complex Self
(externalities)

Agent Self
(power of choice)

In any case, choices of any kind necessarily project outward from the agent self, and so, with or without commitments, you could hardly avoid being involved with externalities. If you were an isolated agent of choice, you would create a world.

In actual fact you are involved with a myriad of other agents of choice and other entities which, although you perceive them by choice, are not there by your initiative.

Your agent self is the one aspect of you that is unambiguously and unavoidably you. Other aspects of you are its doing:

But you do perceive them by choice, since perception depends on an act of attention. Therefore, as part of the environment of your agent self, they are there by your choice. That you should be part of a world which exists without your initiative is itself something you have chosen to be so. You are not a prisoner in it. The "you" that cannot help being part of that system is neither your agent self nor your essential self, but your complex self. But this would not be "you" except for the identification with it which is the act of your agent self. Your agent self is the one aspect of you that is unambiguously and unavoidably "you". The other aspects of the self are its doing. *Living is something you do, not something that happens to you.*

Above, we have depicted the three aspects of the self as the three sides of a triangle. This represents the fact that each aspect is intimately related to each of the others. This simple model will help us to see what the alternatives are for a basic life policy.

11 Basic Life Policies

What would a basic life policy be? What is basic in life? Life is an interaction among living beings and between them and non-living things. Therefore, a basic life policy is one that specifies the basic character of that relationship so far as your own conduct is concerned.

Your basic life policy specifies your relationship policy with the community of living beings:

Now, the way you treat non-living things depends on the way you treat living beings. This is because living beings have a common interest in the same non-living things, and non-living things do not have interests of their own (if you thought they did you would call them living). Therefore, a basic life policy will be a policy concerning your relationship to the community of living beings.

Of course, your relationship with the living community is itself governed by many levels of intention. Your basic life policy will concern the highest level, the most basic characteristics of that relationship.

The questions to be resolved are at the level of cooperation vs. competition. However, these concepts are too ambiguous to be of much help in analyzing basic life policies. The key for clarifying cooperation vs. competition is the threefold analysis of the self. That analysis applies to living beings generally. They have the power of choice, which is primarily what we mean by living. They have commitments which define their basic ways of living (we may call these instincts or even mechanisms, but in any case they are commitments). And they have involvements with externalities. The externalities constitute the arena in which living beings interact. But a basic life policy will deal not only with that but also with your attitude to the other two aspects of the self, both as regards your own self and also other selves.

I am not saying that every living being has a basic life policy. Far from it. Many human beings do not seem for the most part to have any basic life policy. They act on policies that are at this basic level, but they sometimes act on one policy, sometimes on another, and they usually do not act on them *as policies*. They think of them as aspects of human nature for the most part, and sometimes adopt them as policies but seldom very consistently.

Basic life policies are not descriptions of human nature or personality types:

So the point of discussing basic life policies is not to describe human nature, nor yet to describe various personality types, but rather to raise your consciousness concerning these issues so as to enable you to put your essential self into better shape. If you have a basic life policy it will be part of your essential self, since it will be a commitment, and it will be your supreme commitment as regards your relationships, But of course your essential self will include much more than that as well.

For the moment I leave it open whether it is wise to have a basic life policy or not. In this chapter, I will not answer that question, but only show you what the alternative basic life policies are.

Your basic life policies depend on your conception of yourself and others:

Basic life policies correspond to the degree and kind of interest you take in the three aspects of the self respectively. They depend on your conception of yourself and others and your attitude to that conception. You may think of yourself and others mainly in terms of externalities, or mainly in terms of commitments, or mainly as agents of choice, or a combination of these. And you may either accept or reject that aspect of the self or those aspects of the self which you mainly think of. The aspect or aspects, which you do not think of as part of the self, you have already rejected from the field of your attention, so you do not need to adopt an *attitude* of acceptance or rejection with respect to them.

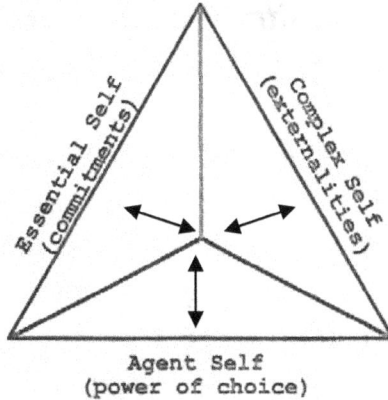

Essential Self
(commitments)

Complex Self
(externalities)

Agent Self
(power of choice)

To represent all this in a revealing way, we will elaborate the triangle representing the threefold self. Think of that triangle as the base of a three-sided pyramid (viewed from above). If you are on one of the slopes of the pyramid, you cannot see the other two slopes. This means thinking of the self in terms of that one aspect and neglecting the other two. Your distance down from the ridge is the degree to which you neglect or ignore the aspect on the other side. If you are on one of the ridges, you can see two of the slopes but not the third. This means thinking of the self in terms of both of those aspects and ignoring the third. Your distance down from the peak is the degree to which you ignore the third aspect. If you are on the peak, you can see all three of the slopes. This means thinking of the self in terms of all three aspects.

Thus, your position on the pyramid represents your way of thinking about the aspects of the self. If this is distorted, it will not correspond to your actual involvement with the three aspects. These aspects all remain parts of the self, whether you think they are or not. If you pretend that some aspect is not part of the self, it continues to function as such but goes "underground" and functions badly as a result.

You choices, commitments, and externalities are part of you whether you think they are or not:

For example, if you deny the power of choice, you are still doing what you do by choice, but without the benefit of reasons that are clearly considered. If you deny the element of commitments, you will probably still have commitments, but they will probably not be consistent and you will probably not act consistently with them. If you deny that externalities are part of the self, you will not be less involved in them, but you will probably abuse them and be abused by them.

Your conceptions of the self and your attitudes to aspects of it are interdependent. This is because the aspects of the self, unlike many other things, are plain for you to see at all times, being part of you. Furthermore, their essential interdependence is also plainly before you at all times. If you think of any two of them interacting, the third automatically comes into the picture.

Without conscious consideration, the three aspects of self will not function properly:

If you think of the power of choice in relation to externalities, the continuity of those externalities and their involvement of other individuals calls for some continuity in your choices, therefore commitments. If you think of the power of choice in relation to commitments, externalities are automatically brought into the picture to make sense of these commitments. If you think of commitments in relation to externalities, that is, externalities as another aspect of the self, the power of choice is automatically brought into the picture because the variety and richness of the externalities require many choices that are not determined by your commitments.

It follows that if you try to think of the self in terms of two of its aspects, leaving out the third, you cannot fully accept even those two as aspects of the self, and the more completely you try to shut out the third, the more you must despise the two in terms of which you conceive the self. There is therefore ambivalence or a conflict involved in this attempt.

However, if you single out just one aspect of the self and make that your whole conception of the self, you can fully accept it, since you are not thinking of its interaction with any other part of the self. The other two aspects then are simply seen as not your concern but only occasions to react to or tools to make use of.

These facts are reflected in the pyramid model. To think of one of the three aspects as part of the self, means being on that slope or along its border. To fully accept that aspect of the self as part of the self is to be on the centre line of that slope (vertically down from the peak). To be partway from there to the corner is to have an ambivalent or halfhearted attitude to that aspect as part of the self. To be right at the corner is to reject it while at the same time conceiving the self in that way.

Full
acceptance _____   _____ Rejection

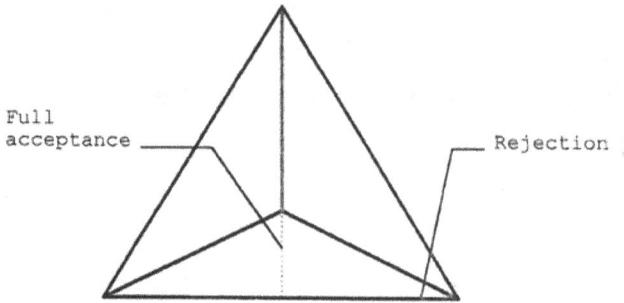

To think of the self in terms of two aspects, ignoring the third, is to be down on one ridge, and this takes you off-centre on both of those slopes. This is therefore an ambivalent or conflicting outlook. But you can be down on the centre line of one slope, thus fully accepting one aspect while ignoring the other two.

From these observations, you can see that only the peak of the pyramid represents an accurate conception of the self. Only from that point of view is it possible to have a basic life policy that will fully serve your true interest. The further you get from the peak the less adequate will the corresponding basic life policy be for serving your true interest. Let us now survey a number of key positions on the pyramid and the basic life policies that fit those conceptions of the self and attitudes to the self.

Life policies that focus on externalities:

We begin with the side of externalities, since this is the main emphasis found in our society. We are now looking at the pyramid from that side. Over the two horizons are the other two aspects of the self.

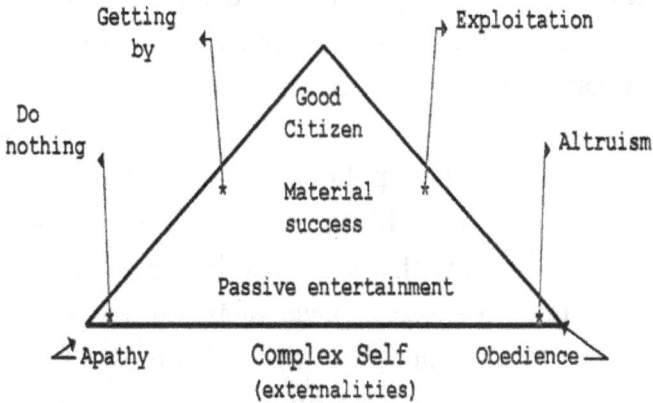

Passive Entertainment – A policy that only recognizes externalities as an aspect of the self:

Let us move up the centre from the bottom. At the bottom, we have a policy that ignores both the power of choice and commitments completely and completely accepts externalities as the only aspect of the self. I will call this policy "passive entertainment." This person is a cork bobbing on the ocean of material and social happenings, passive because of ignoring the power of choice, and seeing life merely as entertainment, because of ignoring commitments.

Material Success – A policy that recognizes choices and commitments only grudgingly as aspects of self with externalities being of central interest:

Halfway up the centre line we have a similar interest, but with a somewhat grudging recognition of the power of choice and commitments. This is the stereotype of a policy of "material success." The initiatives and commitments needed to provide comforts and entertainments are accepted only because they are necessary and only to that extent, not as part of the self. This seems to be the policy of those people who have a job only in order to make enough money to keep an apartment and pay for "living it up" on weekends and vacations. Notice that a policy of material success is not necessarily the one most likely to actually result in material success. The difficulty with a policy of this sort is that it takes a grudging attitude to those aspects of the self which must be brought into action if success is to be ensured. This is all the more true of passive entertainment, where the goods are expected to drop into one's lap, so to speak. This person needs a lot of luck to succeed, quite apart from the question of whether success in such a policy would constitute a satisfying life.

Good Citizen – A policy that recognizes all three aspects of self as important, but externalities are most important:

Moving on up close to the peak, we have the popular conception of a "good citizen." This is still basically a "materialistic" policy, but now the other two aspects of the self are recognized as important, though not on a par with externalities. Success is still conceived in terms of externalities: house, pleasant neighbors, good job, respectable status, and the like. The power of choice and commitments are recognized as important but not quite seen as aspects of the self.

Further implications for other locations on this depiction of the Complex Self may be seen in Appendix 1.

Life policies that focus on commitments:

We move now to the side of the essential self by considering the following diagram showing the face of our pyramid containing only the essential self.

Blind Obsession – A policy that ignores choice and externalities aspects of one's self with total focus on commitments:

Following the same procedure as before, we begin at bottom centre. This is a policy totally dominated by commitments and giving no recognition to externalities or the power of choice. This is therefore a policy of blind obsession. It is blind because any reason for the commitments would have to be found in the other aspects of oneself and other selves. There is a quality of madness here, and such persons are likely to find their way to a mental hospital. But if the obsession is such that they can draw others into it, then madness may even become law.

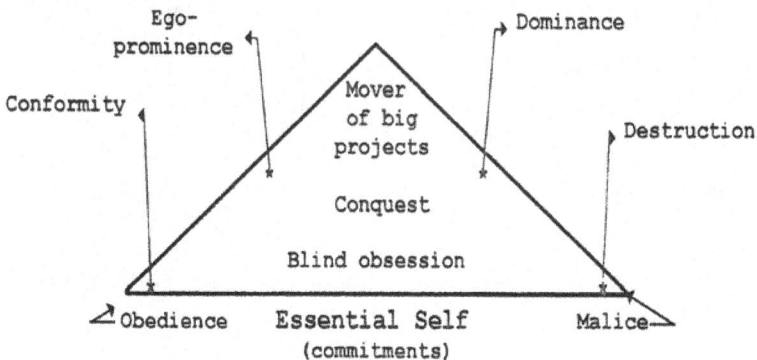

Conquest – A policy that recognizes choices and externalities only grudgingly as aspects of self with commitment being of central interest:

Moving halfway up the centre, we have a similar policy but with some color of rationality because there is some recognition of the other aspects of the self. This person is much more likely to gain the cooperation or acquiescence of others. I call this a policy of conquest, because the stereotypes are the charismatic leaders who carry everything before them — the Napoleons and Hitlers for example.

Mover of Big Projects - A policy that recognizes all three aspects of self as important, but commitment is of central importance:

Moving up near the peak, we have the recognition of the other aspects of the self as significant but not quite as parts of the self. These people, when successful, are the movers of big projects, often of great benefit to society, yet tending to have their own momentum in disregard of the question of benefit.

Further implications for other locations on this depiction of the Essential Self may be seen in Appendix 1.

Life policies that focus on choice:

We turn now to the third side of the pyramid, the side of the agent self.

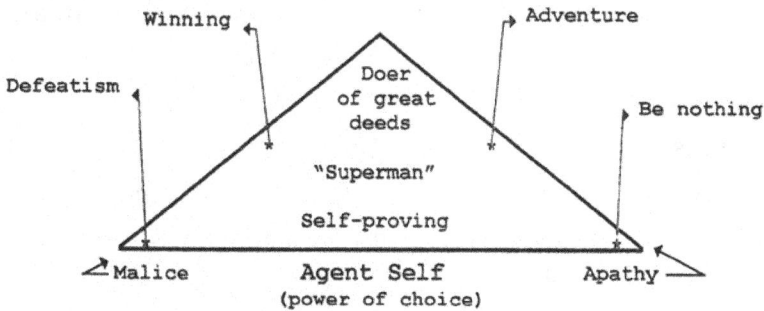

Self-Proving – A policy focused on the power of choice for the sake of being able to choose, without regard for what is chosen:

Again, starting at bottom centre, we have the complete acceptance of the power of choice, and the rejection of commitments and externalities as aspects of the self. This policy is similar to blind obsession in lacking any reason for its concrete content. It is a policy of demonstrating the power of choice for the sake of doing so, without any concern about one deed being any more worthwhile than another is, except that it shows the power of choice. In other words, it is a policy of proving oneself, in the sense of proving what you can do, with a similar interest in what others can do.

Superman – A policy of self-proving with no sense of limitation, but in the context of the social and physical order of things:

Moving halfway up the centre, we now have a partial recognition of the other aspects of the self. This is still a policy of self-proving, but within the context of the social and physical order of things. This imposes the necessity of more meaningful and demanding demonstrations of oneself, and so I call this the "superman" policy. People who think of themselves in these terms have little or no sense of their own limitations, since the idea that they have limitations is taboo. Therefore, they carry on beyond their limitations, repressing all warning signs, until something breaks.

Doer of Great Deeds – A policy taking into account commitments and externalities, but attaching exaggerated importance of demonstrating one's power of choice:

Moving on up near the peak, we have a similar outlook, but now commitments and externalities are recognized as important, though not as parts of the self. This is a policy of doing great deeds, and people with this outlook may indeed do important things that others would not do. Still, they are apt to misjudge the importance of those deeds because of attaching an exaggerated importance to demonstrating the power of choice and not giving enough consideration to commitments and externalities.

Further implications for other locations on this depiction of the Agent Self may be seen in Appendix 1.

One key position remains, and this is the very peak of the pyramid. This point is dead centre relative to all three sides, and is the one point from which all sides are fully in view. This policy involves a full and equal acceptance of all three aspects of the self as being important for their own sakes.

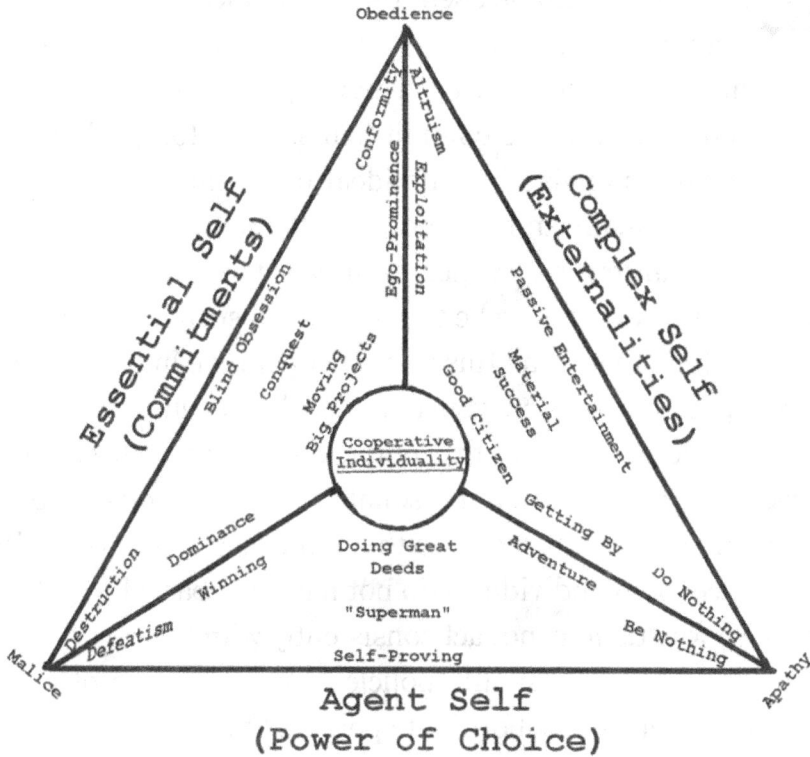

Cooperative Individuality: A policy of accepting choice, commitments & externalities as fully important parts of one self as well as recognition that we share with others the value of externalities.

To accept this both for oneself and for others has important implications. The complex self is not something exclusive to any one individual but is shared by many, though with many points of view and different emphases.

The essential self takes its particular form in terms of the complex self and in the light of the full acceptance of many agent selves and many distinctive essential selves. Because of

65

the sharing of the complex self, the acceptance of many agent and essential selves amounts to the acceptance of a community of individuals, each having its unique power of choice and its distinctive commitments. Therefore, this point of view involves envisaging the ideal of all these individuals working individually and cooperatively to maintain a system of externalities in terms of which each can develop most richly. The policy must therefore be to take part in such a community and contribute to it. I call this policy cooperative individuality.

Now, let me remind you that this has been a survey of basic life policies, with the emphasis on both basic and policies. These are not personality types, though some personality types correspond to then. They are not personality types, since many individuals do not have any basic life policy, and those who do may not act consistently with them.

Also, these are basic life policies. To act on one of them may involve forming subordinate policies that would resemble one or more of the other policies in the continuum, but would not have the status of basic policies. For example, if your basic policy is cooperative individuality, its implementation may involve being a good citizen in the conventional sense. However, this subordinate 'good citizen' policy will not be quite like the basic "good citizen" policy, since it will spring from a more balanced and integrated point of view.

If your basic policy is exploitation, the implementation of this may also involve adopting a "good citizen" policy as a means. But here again the subordinate "good citizen" policy will not be quite like the *basic* "good citizen" policy. In this case, it will be distorted in the direction of being a front to gain the cooperation of others so as to better exploit them.

But most people, it seems, do not have *any* basic life policy. One or two basic policies may predominate in their outlook, but they do not adopt any one as the guiding principle of their lives. Instead, they skip around from one mode of behaviour to another, according to the stimulus offered by the occasion. When irritated, they may momentarily indulge in malice. In a time of crisis, they may do a great deed. When they sit down in front of their television set, they may give way to passive entertainment. When they think of investing their money or applying for a job, they may think in terms of exploitation or material success. At times, for example on the arrival of a child in the family, they may adopt the outlook of cooperative individuality.

You may find it instructive to examine your own personality in terms of this model. Perhaps you will find things you do not like and have not paid attention to before. Perhaps also you will find things that give you a more favorable view of yourself than you had.

From the survey of basic life policies it will be clear that cooperative individuality is inherently superior to all the others. And it will perhaps be clear that the further away from the peak you go, the less healthy the policies become. What has not been made clear is what the implication of this is as to how you should live. Should you have one single basic life policy and live consistently by that, or should you skip around amongst them giving emphasis to some of the ones not too far from the peak? These are the questions to be answered in the following chapters.

12 A Supreme Value

Why should you adopt one basic life policy rather than another? If there is to be a reason, it must rest on something more fundamental than any particular basic life policy. There must be a value to be served, and it must be served more effectively by one policy than any other. Moreover, this value must be worthy of being adopted as your supreme value, meaning the value that governs all your actions. Otherwise it will not suffice for deciding the issue of basic life policies. Is there such a value? If there is, it must be able to pass certain tests, in particular, the following.

Why satisfaction qualifies as your supreme life value:

1. It must recommend itself to your intuitive sense of value; in other words, it must be attractive and seem right.

2. You must not need to ignore or distort any aspect of your own nature in order to accept it. An accurate view of the self must not generate misgivings about it.

3. It must stand up to use. Living by it must not lead to disillusionment but rather reinforce your intuitive sense of its rightness.

We can immediately draw out some implications of these three requirements.

a. It must be compatible with enjoyment and contentment. If it were not, it would not recommend itself to your intuitive sense of value, at least not in the long run, and not if you are taking all aspects of your own nature into account.

b. You must not need to ignore or distort any aspect of the self in order to actually live by it. This follows from #2 and #3.

c. It must be incompatible with regret, discontentment, and depression. Its acceptance as a value must imply the rejection of these, and consistently living by it must entail living so as to avoid these. This follows from #1 and #3.

Now, think of a scale going from a state of regret to the diametrical opposite of regret and extending beyond these to more extreme states in both directions. What is the diametrical opposite of regret?

Since regret is a feeling you have towards your deeds or the situation you are involved in, its opposite will be the opposite feeling aroused by these same things. Such a feeling is the feeling of satisfaction.

Satisfaction is a sense of well-being in the face of your choices and your situation (which comprise your essential and complex selves). It depends on being aware of where you are and what you are doing, and of the significance of these. In this respect it is like regret. It is not the same as pleasure.

How satisfaction is different than pleasure:

Some pleasures can only be enjoyed if you close your eyes to some aspects of where you are and what you are doing; to contemplate the full moral significance of them would spoil them, for example, eating food that isn't good for you, but tastes good. The opposite is true of satisfaction.

You may avoid regret by ignoring the significance of what you are doing; but you will not thereby gain satisfaction. Satisfaction is not a fruit of self-deception. It comes from being objective about your choices and your situation and finding them worthy *of* your approval – to your satisfaction. You can experience this when you would not experience pleasure. For example, if you help out someone who is seriously injured, you will hardly find pleasure in doing so, but you can take satisfaction in it.

Ultimate satisfaction is joy:

When your satisfaction is full and overflowing, the word for this is joy. Joy is found when your own deeds and the life around you achieve a harmony that abounds with vitality. The laughter of happy children gives us joy. True friendship gives us joy. Shared endeavors with a worthwhile purpose give us joy.

Joy and heartsickness are extreme opposites:

At the opposite extreme, when you are crushed by an overwhelming regret, you experience heartsickness. When someone you love falls into evil ways, when your friend betrays you, and most of all when you know you have betrayed your friends, heartsickness is then your intimate companion.

HEARTSICKNESS---REGRET--- SATISFACTION---JOY

When your experience is dominated by regret, you experience discontentment. When your experience would be dominated by regret if you were facing the facts, you also experience discontentment. In the latter case you may wonder why you are discontented. In your reluctance to admit that the cause is within yourself, you may look for causes supposedly beyond your control. This allows you to feel sorry for yourself and perhaps indulge in the palliative of indignation against others. But such a response only heightens your discontentment.

Having cause for regret may not be the only source of discontentment. But since cause for regret is sufficient cause for discontentment, it follows that you cannot experience contentment unless you have cause for satisfaction. Just as an unexplained discontentment is a warning sign that you probably need to change your ways or your outlook, so an unexplained contentment is a sign that you are doing things the right way but are not giving yourself credit. Consequently, you are denying yourself the experience of satisfaction and perhaps joy.

Another opposite of joy is depression.

HEARTSICKNESS---REGRET--- SATISFACTION---JOY

DEPRESSION---DISCONTENTMENT---CONTENTMENT

Depression is the sign that your vital powers are not being exercised. This may have its basis in lack of opportunity, or malnutrition, or fatigue, as well as an unwholesome outlook or unwholesome habits. But in any case it indicates that some transformation either in your situation or your intentions is called for. But unlike regret and heartsickness, it does not tell you what change is needed. It is therefore similar to discontentment, but further removed from joy, since discontentment has the stirrings of vitality in it, though without adequate direction.

In the light of all this, think about satisfaction in connection with what is required of a value that would govern all your actions.

1. Satisfaction is compatible with enjoyment and contentment.
2. To pursue satisfaction as a value you do not need to ignore or distort any aspect of the self. On the contrary, the experience of satisfaction depends on awareness of your power of choice, your commitments, and the complex self.
3. Satisfaction is incompatible with regret, depression, and discontentment. Its acceptance as a value implies the rejection of these, and living so as to achieve it entails living so as to avoid these.
4. Satisfaction recommends itself to our intuitive sense of value. It is attractive. By the very nature of what affords

satisfaction, satisfaction must seem right, since it depends on a state of the self which seems right.

5. Considering satisfaction in the light of an accurate conception of the self will not generate misgivings about one's self. On the contrary, its pursuit depends on cultivating an accurate conception of the self.

6. Satisfaction will stand up to use. To live by it is to cultivate those intentions and situations that will give you a sense of things being right in so far as you are involved. Consequently, its tendency is towards the opposite of disillusionment. Its pursuit tends to reinforce the sense of its rightness.

I have just enumerated the requirements for a supreme value and shown that satisfaction fulfills them all. However, this does not add up to a proof, and so, to strengthen the case somewhat, I will answer two objections that represent the thinking of a good many people.

Objection 1: There are those who think that the goods of life have nothing to do with regret or its opposite. These are of the opinion that to enjoy the goods of life it is all the more efficient to blind yourself to questions of whether things seem right or not. Such questions, they think, are only an impediment to enjoyment.

To these I answer that they are not facing the facts of life. You may have a brief period of enjoyment in disregard of questions of right and wrong, but when you do what *would* seem wrong *if* you were facing all the facts, you cannot escape discontentment or depression. If you habitually ignore questions of right and wrong, on the premise that they interfere with enjoyment, then your policy is such as to incur an ever-deepening discontentment or depression. But discontentment and depression are incompatible with enjoyment. Therefore, I say that this outlook cannot succeed in its purpose, and when it is corrected so as to take account of the facts, there is no longer any objection to satisfaction as a supreme value.

Objection 2: There are those who think that for a *supreme* value the question of contentment and enjoyment is irrelevant. They will concede that satisfaction has been shown to be acceptable as a value, but not as a supreme value. A supreme value, they think, must depend on rightness alone.

Those who think in this way are overlooking the requirement that a supreme value should stand up to use. If your supreme value gives no weight to enjoyment and contentment, you are incurring the risk that living by it will lead to disillusionment. Therefore, by saying that enjoyment and contentment are not relevant, you do not strengthen your devotion to what is right. On the contrary, you weaken it. To be consistent with thinking that right and wrong are the supreme issues, you should adopt satisfaction as your supreme value.

Can we go on to show that satisfaction is the *only* value that can pass the test of a supreme value? *The* reasons already given imply that if there is another value that can pass the test, its achievement would include the achievement of satisfaction. But satisfaction has the advantage that the very concept of it is rooted in the requirements for a supreme value. This means that in taking satisfaction as the supreme value you are not in danger of being misled. For example, values rooted in religious concepts, such as the love of God, are subject to grave misinterpretations. It may be that when properly understood, such a value is worthy of being supreme. But how would you know you were properly interpreting the love of God as a guide to action? Would you not have to determine that your way of understanding it would actually lead you to actions on which you could look with approval when their full nature was before your mind? But to do this would be to take satisfaction as your criterion for interpreting this other supreme value.

In other words, the only way you can replace satisfaction with some other value is by doing so only nominally, while the operative value is satisfaction. This is not a gain but a loss, since you have lost something in the way of clarity.

At this point a reminder is in order. With all this talk of *doing* what is right, some readers may have forgotten that regret and satisfaction do not only concern the rightness or wrongness of your own deeds, You can regret what someone else does, provided it is someone you identify with. You can regret the situation you are in. And you can take satisfaction from these things. So in recommending satisfaction as the supreme value I am referring to the sense of rightness *of the whole self*, including the complex self. "Fullness of life" is another phrase for such a state of rightness. One might suggest fullness of life as the supreme value, but if you were to ask why, a reasonable answer would be, because it satisfies. Therefore, satisfaction seems to take precedence.

But, you may say, why not take joy rather than mere satisfaction as the supreme value? I would say yes to this, except that joy is sometimes only a remote prospect, no matter how adequate your guidelines are. But if you have adequate guidelines, satisfaction is always attainable, at least with regard to your own acts of choice. Moreover, joy is only the abundance of satisfaction, so that if satisfaction is your supreme value, you will not fail to pursue joy when there is any prospect of attaining it.

I will continue, then, on the assumption that we have accepted satisfaction as the supreme value, the value that should govern all our acts of choice.

13 A Life Policy that Satisfies

Satisfaction depends on having a clear view of your situation and your acts of choice. If you think of this in connection with the threefold analysis of the self, you can see that a view of yourself and others that takes full account of all three aspects will be the most helpful in pursuing satisfaction. The basic life policy of cooperative individuality is the only one that accords with such a view of the self.

Consider once again what such a policy amounts to. "This point of view involves envisaging the ideal of all these individuals working individually and cooperatively to maintain a system of externalities in terms of which each can develop most richly. The policy must therefore be to take part in such a community and contribute to it. I call this policy cooperative individuality."

Notice that although this policy has an altruistic side to it, it is misleading to call it an altruistic policy. It is a policy of *being part of* a community. This means both making one's contribution to it and benefiting from it. The ideal that *each* should develop most richly includes oneself in the same way as it includes the others.

If you think about satisfaction, you can see that if you exclude yourself from being a beneficiary, if you think of doing what is right exclusively in terms of doing things for the benefit of others, the satisfaction to be gained from such deeds goes sour. Such a concept of what is right would not stand up to use, at least not if your mind was open to a balanced concept of yourself and others. What is special about you that everyone except you alone should be a beneficiary? The nature of things provides no support for such a view.

Furthermore, a purely altruistic policy implies that you are not worthy to receive benefits. This means that you are not granting to others the privilege of benefiting you. And so what you regard as virtuous in yourself you are denying to others. Therefore, you are not treating them with respect. Disrespect for yourself precludes respect for others. For this reason pure altruism is an outlook in conflict with itself, since it is an attempt to respect others while not permitting them to respect you. To pursue it you must reduce your concept of others to one that would fit a policy of passive entertainment on their part.

On the other hand, if you try to conceive of benefits as applying exclusively to yourself, not to others, you cannot then think of yourself as part of a community at all. Your concept of the benefits to be obtained cannot consistently include those of shared pleasures, shared endeavors, or mutual respect, friendship, or love.

If you try to conceive of benefits as applying exclusively to you, you cannot take the balanced view of yourself represented by the peak of the pyramid, for that requires seeing the externalities as a complex self shared by many individuals. Each individual participates in it in its unique way, but on the basis of the same threefold structure of the self. You would need to go down the slope in one direction or another.

You may go down on the externalities side, in which case your concept of benefits for yourself is degraded so that what you do is no longer a major ingredient in your concept of benefits, but only what happens to you. On this basis you cannot gain satisfaction, for living is primarily what you do.

If you try the commitments side, you must either settle for a meaningless obsession or see your benefits in the contrast between yourself and others, as in ego-prominence or dominance. None of these has positive benefit in the picture, but at most a negative effect on others.

If you try the agent side, you must either settle for meaningless exercises of the power of choice, or the viewpoint of a policy of adventure, which merely mixes meaningless exercises of choice with something like passive entertainment. Or go in the direction of winning, which again treats benefits in terms of the contrast between yourself and others, another negative approach.

In all these alternatives, the concept of benefit either has no positive content, or its content involves only what happens to you. Therefore, there is no prospect of satisfaction in any of them.

All this is by way of clarifying what it means to do what is right, and correcting the common traditional views. The champions of egoism think they are being practical, but in fact, one who lives by that principle is doing himself no favor. The champions of altruism think they are recommending high principles of virtue, but in fact, one who lives by that principle is doing others no favor. Neither of these principles does what it is supposed to do when put into practice.

The renaming principle is that of community. According to this principle, what benefits you benefits others, and what benefits others benefits you. This does not mean that your benefits are identical with the benefits of others, but only that they go hand in hand. The reason they do is quite simple. The complex self, the external aspects of the self, bodies, houses, trees, are not possessed exclusively by any one individual. The manner of possession varies, but possession in one manner or another is shared.

Even if you are so isolated from other human beings that you can leave them out of the picture, you are certainly not isolated from all living things. You depend on them for the maintenance of your physical life.

You may think you possess your body exclusively, but this is not so, since it is part of the experience of others, though in a different way. You may have certain very private possessions that no one else sees, perhaps a diary or a letter. But these articles, through their influence on your personality, are indirectly part of the experience of others as well.

When you try to possess something exclusively (not just privately) what are you doing? If you could succeed in shutting it off from the experience of others, you would, to that extent, shut yourself off from others. This could not enrich your experience. At most it would make the experience of others poorer. So this approach, if it could succeed, would be futile. The remaining way in which you might try to possess something exclusively would be to make it of no benefit to others, but only to yourself. This would be adding malice to egoism.

You are therefore stuck, whether you like it or not, with the principle of community as the only practical principle. If you have misgivings about it, perhaps this is because it seems to imply that there would be no privacy and no private ownership, no special "territory" to call your own. However, it does not imply this. Two cardinal points should be noticed.

1. To say that your benefits and the benefits of others go hand in hand is not to say that your benefits are the same as the benefits of others.

2. To say that you do not possess any of the external things exclusively is not to say that you do not possess any of them in a special way, nor is it to say that you do not possess any of them privately. Private possession is not exclusive possession, as I pointed out earlier.

The implication of the principle of community with regard to private possessions and private "territory" is this; these things by benefiting you should also benefit others, and if they do not benefit others they will not genuinely benefit you. How can they benefit others? By enriching your life in such a way that your life enriches other lives.

If your life is truly enriched it will enrich others. Why is this so? Because it will then be a part of the complex self of others as an enriching factor. This must be so, since if your life is set against other lives, through policies such as exploitation, ego-prominence, dominance, or winning, your own life will be impoverished. If you try to isolate your life from others, your life will be impoverished. If you try to act so that it makes no difference what the effect on other lives is, as in policies of passive entertainment, blind obsession, and self-proving, your life is impoverished.

You can not enrich your life without enriching others:

There is no alternative except cooperative individuality or something close to it, and this has the effect of enriching other lives. The more you depart from cooperative individuality the more you tend to impoverish your own life. Therefore, you cannot enrich your own life without also enriching other lives. Moreover, since you are not likely to enrich other lives without intending to do so, the only policies that can be counted on to enrich your own life are those that aim at enriching both your life and others. The only basic life policy that has this as a clear aim is cooperative individuality.

In cooperative individuality, individuality is just as important as cooperation. If you think of the threefold self, a full recognition of the agent self and the essential self implies a policy of individuality. The uniqueness and autonomy of the individual cannot be avoided if you keep both these aspects in mind. This is because the essential self is the work of the agent of choice, not some outside force. To escape from recognizing this you must move in the direction of leaving the agent self out of the picture. But if the agent self is fully recognized and the uniqueness of the essential self is recognized, you cannot avoid recognizing the unique manner of possessing externalities, that is, the uniqueness of the complex self.

Cooperation implies individuality:

Indeed, cooperation implies individuality, if cooperation is understood as being directed at the common benefit. This follows from what has been said, since the only common benefit that is possible is one that applies in a unique way to each individual. Each individual must benefit in a unique way. Common cannot mean uniform. Moreover, the only way in which everyone can cooperate so as to benefit everyone is for each one to contribute in a unique way. This follows from the analysis of the self and the survey of basic life policies. Regimenting or conditioning the masses into a uniform contribution will not work. It will destroy the self, and no one will benefit.

Therefore, the only true community is a community of unique individuals, none subservient to any others, and each living for the benefit of all, each self included. This leaves us with cooperative individuality as the only basic life policy that can adequately serve the supreme value of satisfaction.

At this point, a common response will be to say, yes, cooperative individuality is very good as an overall policy, but it is very idealistic. You can't change human nature, and in everyday living there has to be a little bit of passive entertainment, a bit of exploitation, a bit of ego-prominence, a bit of winning, and so forth. Anyway, there is no harm done so long as your main approach is cooperative individuality.

My answer is that this is a very sloppy way of thinking. If you base your life on this way of thinking you will never achieve the level of satisfaction you are capable of. My purpose is to show you how you can attain a life of almost unbroken satisfaction. And with a bit of luck a life mainly of joy.

But we must unscramble some ideas and begin to think clearly.

First of all, let us recognize that none of us will ever be flawless. Reality is too intricate for this to be possible. And who would have it otherwise? If reality were so simple and bland as to permit the flawless carrying out of a basic life policy, it would be uninteresting and would not provide the potentiality for a really full life.

Making mistakes doesn't imply one shouldn't try to make each move count for the best:

But to say that we will make mistakes and sometimes slip from the policy we have set ourselves is no argument for compromising the policy. A chess player intends every move to count towards winning, but he knows very well that he will not always succeed in this. This does not mean he should compromise his policy and follow a policy of just making most of his moves count.

In the same way, the fact that we have tendencies towards malice or exploitations for example, and will sometimes slip into these patterns of behaviour, does not mean that our *policy* should have a place in it for these patterns.

Repression of impulses is not correction:

We do have impulses and feelings that run counter to the policy of cooperative individuality. Having a policy of cooperative individuality does not mean you should repress those impulses and feelings and try to pretend they do not exist. This would accomplish nothing. Repressed impulses and feelings do not go away. They manifest themselves in other less recognizable forms. *Repression is not correction.* You should keep all these wayward impulses and feelings out in the open where you can deal with them constructively and keep them from interfering with the carrying out of your policy.

Nor does a policy of cooperative individuality mean you should condemn yourself whenever you deviate from it or are inclined to do so. Condemning yourself only makes you less capable of learning from experience. *Condemnation is not correction.* You will never be flawless, so why worry about it? But learn from experience and keep to the best policy.

In suggesting that cooperative individuality should be your exclusive policy, remember that we are talking here only about basic life policies, not about the activities by which you might implement such a policy. In carrying out a policy of cooperative individuality, you might find it expedient to do things that would superficially look like some other basic life policy if they were misunderstood. If the surgeon's work were not seen in its total context, one might think he was acting maliciously. In general, cooperative individuality would not lead one to cut someone's body open. But under the circumstances in which the surgeon does this, it might.

So when I suggest an exclusive policy of cooperative individuality, I am not suggesting that all your actions should be nice. Nor am I saying you should never win, or never be prominent in society, or not be materially successful, or never have adventure. There is nothing wrong with these things, as parts of a life of cooperative individuality. But as basic life policies they are inadequate.

Imagination helps us explore possibilities:

And last but not least, we should remember that fantasy is an important element in life. Through fantasy, we can explore the implications of various basic life policies without putting them into actual practice. Good stories serve this purpose. A good story is always a story about basic life policies in one form or another, and a believable story tells the truth about what will satisfy and what will not.

Other forms of fantasy serve the same purpose, though not all fantasy deals with basic life policies. It is important to recognize that representing unacceptable behaviour in fantasy is not itself unacceptable behavior. It is possible to indulge those impulses that are contrary to cooperative individuality through jokes, sports, and games without actually deviating from the policy. For, in these play activities, if you maintain the spirit of fantasy and do not allow it to become "serious", the play activity is in accordance with cooperative individuality although what is represented in it may not be.

The same is true in reading a story. You can enjoy reading about wicked deeds without having any intention, or even inclination, to commit then yourself. So, far from suggesting that these wayward feelings and impulses should be eliminated from life altogether (which is impossible), I am suggesting that they should be kept in the forefront of attention through the various forms of fantasy. We keep reminding ourselves of their true nature and consequences through stories and so are less tempted to exercise them in real life.

Now I will explain in positive terms why you ought to maintain an exclusive policy of cooperative individuality.

There is a habit-forming tendency which affects all our activities, whether of thought or of action. Whatever kinds of choices you make becomes a little easier to make those kinds of choices again. Whatever kinds of choices you reject, it becomes a little easier to reject those kinds of choices again and a little more difficult to *make* those kinds of choices.

In particular, whatever conception of yourself you entertain (not in fantasy but in real application), it becomes easier to entertain it again, and it becomes more difficult to entertain other conceptions inconsistent with it.

In other words, in living, as in sports or in any craft, there is a factor of training. You are good at what you are in training for, and you are not good at what you are out of training for. If you do things that are contrary to the state of training you would like to be in, your state of training is impaired.

Now, I have shown why cooperative individuality is the only basic life policy that fits with an adequate conception of yourself and others. And I have shown why only an adequate conception of the self, giving full status to all three aspects of your self, makes a satisfying life possible. Any indulgence in other basic life policies will involve thinking of yourself and others in ways that do not take full account of all three aspects of the self. This will make it more difficult to think of yourself and others in terms of all three aspects of the self. It will undermine the state of training which makes a satisfying life feasible.

Being careful to always apply a life policy helps make it a habit:

In other words, you cannot be careless with basic life policies and still live a fully satisfying life. You must stick exclusively to cooperative individuality to do this.

Of course, there are degrees of satisfaction, and you may live a moderately satisfying life by adopting, for example, a policy of the conventional "good citizen," somewhere between cooperative individuality and material success, But satisfaction deserves to be your supreme value, governing all aspects of your life. If you accept this principle, anything less than a completely satisfying life will be to that extent unacceptable. Why settle for anything second-rate when it is within your choice to pursue the best? The best can only be had by adopting cooperative individuality as your exclusive basic life policy.

Such a policy does not imply settling for a monotonous life, one that is virtuous in traditional terms. The survey of basic life policies should have made that clear. The whole point of cooperative individuality is to give the fullest scope to your power of choice through a set of commitments designed to promote and maintain a rich complex self that will serve as the vehicle for a full life in all its natural dimensions.

As you can see, I am implying that the traditional notions of a good or virtuous person are not adequate. We need to develop a new ideal for personal development. This does not mean casting away the old ideals as wrong. It does mean putting them in better perspective and adding neglected dimensions. The core of the new ideal is the full development of the threefold self, the test of which is satisfaction and joy, and the key to which is the basic life policy of cooperative individuality.

14 Priorities for a Way of Life

How to translate these principles into an actual way of life for yourself? This is the question of priorities.

Necessary vs. indispensible activities:

You begin at the top. Ask what activities, what commitments, are indispensable to a truly satisfying life for you. Do not confuse "indispensable" with "necessary." Necessary activities are those that are done for the sake of other things. Washing dishes is necessary so that we can eat under sanitary and appetizing conditions. Sanitary conditions are necessary for the sake of health. But health and eating under appetizing conditions are satisfying in themselves. These are typical of what might be included among the indispensable things (they may or may not be on your particular list).

What is indispensible in your life:

If nothing were worthwhile for its own sake, neither would anything be necessary. Life itself is not necessary unless it holds something desirable for its own sake or can serve something desirable for its own sake. Thus, the indispensable things are those that directly afford satisfaction and are capable of affording joy under favorable conditions.

The indispensable activities, those capable of affording joy, should take priority over the necessary things. This means that you should do the necessary things *in so far as* they serve the indispensable things and *in such a way as* to serve the indispensable things. But you should never let the merely necessary things usurp the place of the indispensable things. Do not make the mistake of the housekeeper who keeps such a spic and span house that people are afraid to enjoy themselves in it. Do not make the mistake of the moralist who is so preoccupied with *duty* that life is preempted of all possible joy, like a squeezed lemon, Duty for what? Is it conceivable that duty itself should be the purpose of life? If so, then what reason could one have for living at all? Why bother with such a life?

Necessity only exists to serve the desirable:

The necessary is necessary only in so far as it serves the desirable. And the only absolutely necessary *is* what serves the indispensable in an essential way.

You begin, then, by determining what is indispensable to a satisfying life for you. Most likely this will encompass some variety. Then you determine what is necessary if these indispensable activities are to be carried out. These are the absolutely necessary activities.

The rule of keeping necessary activity subordinate to the indispensible :

Rule 1: The indispensable and the absolutely necessary form the core of your way of life, with the absolutely necessary kept subordinate to the indispensable.

The rule of frills:

Then there are the desirable but not indispensable activities. We may call these the frills.

Rule 2: Find a place for the frills if you can without interfering with the indispensable things, and therefore without seriously interfering with the absolutely necessary things.

These are the basic rules. Now let us consider how to apply then efficiently, how to get the most mileage out of the arrangement. These three elements, the indispensable, the absolutely necessary, and the frills, are not, or at least need not be, distinct and separate. Some indispensable things may be necessary for the sake of other indispensable things. For example, your indispensables may include exercise, health, and caring for children. Exercise is necessary for health, and health is necessary if you are to care for children. So health and exercise are both indispensable and necessary.

Some necessary things, if done in the right way, may be desirable for themselves. Work, which in principle is done for the sake of other things, can also be satisfying in itself, though not, I suppose, in all cases. The efficient life, in terms of satisfaction, is one in which the conditions of work are arranged so that work is enjoyable.

The rule of efficiency:

For an efficient way of life, then, use the following rule:

Rule 3: As far as possible, do the necessary things in such a way as to convert them into indispensable activities or frills.

In other words, convert as much of life as possible into the category of what is satisfying in itself. What is left over will be either necessary but not desirable for itself (an example might be shaving oneself), or uncontrollable (time unavoidably spent unprofitably, as, for example, waiting in a bus station).

Now, as to the indispensable things. I have described these as capable of affording joy when conditions are favorable, and as giving satisfaction in any case. But let us consider joy, for there is a danger of confusing it with pleasure of the more frivolous sort, Mind you, it is a serious mistake to belittle such pleasures and treat them as only frills, to be fitted in if there is time left over from the "important" things.

I should think that frivolous pleasures deserve a place among the indispensable things, but in any case, they surely deserve a place among the absolutely necessary things because of their contribution to mental health.

Joy in the somber experiences of life including death:

But I want now to consider another mistake, which is to see no joy in the somber experiences of life. Let us consider as an example the death of a loved one, not an untimely or agonizing death, but a quiet death in the fullness of years. This is a sad occasion, but it is a mistake to think of it as a disappointing or grievous one. Death, after all, is universal and not unhealthy. Without death there could not be children, and are not children essential to a human community? Therefore, a normal death in the ripeness of age should be regarded as a normal event, sad because it is a parting, but not unwelcome.

But there is another side to the death of loved ones (and in this category I include friends and neighbors). Such a death draws the community together. It heightens our sense of love for the one who has departed, and also for the friends who remain. One might say that the dead person is more alive after dying than before. Those of us who have experienced this must surely have felt a deep joy, though it may have gone unrecognized. The tears that are shed on such occasions are not all tears of grief, though, alas, most people seen to think they are.

Joy, then, is the same as profound satisfaction. It comes, and can only come, through your full and unstinting participation in the living community. It is with this in mind that you must find the indispensable ingredients of your life. Seek out the things that are indisputably most important to you when the chips are down!

Goals are ends; values apply to means:

Your present life had a beginning, it has a development, and it will have an end. Your priorities are related to that period of time in various ways. Some of the things you are concerned to do are accomplished only as the end result of measures taken, while others are accomplished throughout the process of what is done to accomplish them. The first kind are your *goals*, the second are your *values*.

Examples of goals are buying a house, getting the dishes washed, repairing an appliance, and getting a law enacted. A goal is not accomplished until the process by which it is accomplished is finished, and once a goal is accomplished, the intention to accomplish it becomes inapplicable. It makes no sense to try to buy a house that you have already bought. It makes no sense to wash dishes that have just been properly washed.

Examples of values are taking exercise, playing games, caring for children, and eating good food. The accomplishment of the purpose in the case of a value does not have to wait for the completion of what is done, There is no definite point of completion. You will decide when you have taken enough exercise, but there is no point at which you have taken your exercise, and before which your exercise has not been taken. Running around the block is a goal, since you have not run around the block until you complete the circuit, but running is a value, since you are achieving that purpose all the while you are engaged in the process.

Also, a value remains applicable after it has been achieved. It only becomes temporarily inappropriate. There is no tine at which it is thereafter no longer applicable (unless the conditions change that make it possible). You will still be able to take exercise and there will still be a point in doing so after you have had your exercise for the day. It will still make sense to care for children so long as there are children around.

Goals are not like this. Take the case of washing dishes. Washing dishes, considered as a generality, is a value, in that you can always wash dishes and dishes that should be washed are a recurrent condition. However, washing today's dirty dishes, that is, getting them clean, is a purpose that becomes permanently meaningless once it is accomplished.

Values pertain directly to the quality of life:

Values pertain directly to the quality of life. Goals pertain only indirectly to the quality of life. Let us say you are at this moment acquiring ownership of a house (putting down the final signature). This fact may or may not significantly affect the quality of your life. If it does it will be because of other things consequent upon it, such as living in the house or receiving rent from it. These directly affect the quality of your life. The actual purchase of the house only does so indirectly. Getting the dishes washed is similar. This event in itself does not enter into the quality of your life directly except in the instant of achievement. But it affects it indirectly in the form of the dishes being clean and out of the way, and available for further use.

It is true that the achievement of a goal may be an occasion for celebration, and the satisfaction of achieving the goal may be enjoyed both in anticipation and long after the goal is achieved.

But what makes the goal worth celebrating is the importance of its consequences, not the inherent quality of its being achieved.

By contrast, values represent the very substance of what you consider worthwhile in your life. Eating good food, caring for children, playing games, or for that matter celebration of achieved goals - it is in the doing of such things as these that the satisfactions of life are found, without the necessity of looking beyond them. Therefore, values are what give goals their importance.

The pursuit of a goal, itself, is a value while it is happening:

When you are pursuing a goal, the pursuit of the goal is itself a value. In some cases, the pursuit of a goal is valued for its own sake and not only for the sake of accomplishing the goal. It is conceivable that some people enjoy washing dishes. Also, a goal may be set up for the sake of the value of pursuing it.

Winning is the goal of a game but is not the purpose of playing the game:

This happens in the case of competitive games and sports, if they are played in the right spirit. To play a game properly you must play to win. Winning must be the goal of playing. Yet it is clear that winning a game is not, in general, a goal that contributes to fullness of life. This must be so, since someone must also lose. It is also clear that to play for the sake of winning is to pursue a mistaken basic life policy. Yet to play properly is to play to win.

The answer to this riddle is that winning is the goal of the game but not its purpose. The definition of winning is set up by convention in order to give the game its competitive structure. The competitive structure is what gives the game its peculiar intensity and zest. The purpose of playing should be to enjoy that intensity of effort. To play for the <u>purpose</u> of winning is to pervert the game and degrade the quality of the

97

experience for all those involved. The goal of winning is only a fantasy purpose.

The rule of specific values:

From these considerations, we may draw a very important conclusion that we may set down as the next rule:

Rule 4: Goals should be for the sake of values, and this means values more specific than satisfaction and cooperative individuality.

An important topic in connection with priorities is that of compromises. When values or goals clash, something has to give, so the question arises, how do you decide which values or goals to compromise and in what way?

I have partially answered this question by arguing that satisfaction should be the value that governs all your choices and that cooperative individuality should be your exclusive basic life policy. In other words, these values should never be compromised. This is so because the implication of the argument concerning cooperative individuality is that it will never clash with satisfaction. It may sometimes seem to if you are looking only at the experience of the moment. But if continuity is kept in mind there will not appear to be any conflict.

Satisfaction and cooperative individuality serve as checks on each other, in that by keeping each of them in mind you are protected against drifting into a misconception of the other. Your sense of what cooperative individuality amounts to is kept accurate by remembering that it results in satisfaction. Moreover, you are reminded of what really satisfies by keeping cooperative individuality in mind.

These two values (for cooperative individuality is also a value) are the anchor points for resolving all issues of compromise with regard to other values and goals. All such compromises are made with a view to avoiding any compromise on these. Of course, many other considerations enter into such questions, and some of these will be discussed in the following paragraphs.

The rule of compromise:

But the cardinal rule is:

Rule 5: Decide all compromises of values of goals by the principle that the supreme value of satisfaction and basic life policy of cooperative individuality should never be compromised.

Now I would like to pose the following question:

Why not aim at the best kind of life now:

Why should we not aim at the very best kind of life *now*, instead of in a remote future?

You will say that circumstances do not permit the best kind of life. In a sense, this is true, and in another sense, it is not. It is true that present conditions are surely not the most favorable to joyful living that are possible, at least for many individuals. Nevertheless, let us recall Churchill's statement that the grim days of The Battle of Britain were "their finest hour". He was in effect voicing the principle that living is something you do, not something that happens to you. Sometimes people rise to a fine life under dreadful conditions and sink into decadence under more comfortable conditions.

It raises the question as to what ideal conditions would be, does it not? But to this question there can be no answer, for on the one hand all individuals are different, and on the other hand no individual's life is uniform over time. Furthermore, reality does not include "conditions" as a fixed background against which life is lived. Instead there is the dynamic threefold self, all aspects of which are active and developing. At any moment there is a state of affairs, and life moves on from there.

To live in the best manner is to grasp the finest opportunity that that state of affairs makes possible. This is possible, provided your outlook enables you to do it.

So I ask again, why should we not aim at the best kind of life now? This question comes in the context of having said that life should be dominated by values rather than goals. The fulfillment of values can in principle fill all your tine. Therefore, I ask the question, why should we not aim at the best kind of life now? For, the best kind of life would be one in which time was filled in the best way, that is, in the realization of values of the best kind. Can we not under present conditions live by such values, those of us who are aware of these principles? Living is something you do, not something that happens to you.

Now, we cannot do the same thing all the time, and so the issue arises of the balance of life and the distribution of activities over tine.

Let me repeat the rule of efficiency: As far as possible, do the necessary things in such a way as to convert them into indispensable activities or frills.

We may now add that your understanding of the indispensable activities and the frills, especially the indispensable, should he based on a consideration of the cycles of life, in other words adapted to your own nature as well as the characteristics of the community and the world. In other words, you must think of these values in terms of a *way of life*.

To do justice to this topic would take a book all by itself, but I will only remind you of a few basic points. First of all, you must live your life by the means that are directly available to you. This is the threefold self of the present. You, the agent of choice, do the living. The plan or idea of that life is your structure of commitments, your system of priorities, your essential self. Your immediately available means of realizing that life make up the complex self. This includes your body, your abilities, your status, and the world around you.

This complex self is your instrument for living. It is also the living community apart from your body. You should concern yourself with its care both because of this and because it is your instrument, both for its own sake and as a matter of necessity.

Also included in this complex self are several cycles of time, some provided by nature, some by convention. By nature, we have the seasons of the year, the seasons of the moon, day and night, the biological cycles associated with these, and the life cycle of birth, maturity, and death. By convention, we have the week, the conventions of working hours and mealtimes, and other recurrent occasions such as holidays.

These cycles are resources for living. You should make use of then and not be buffeted about by them.

We are human beings, and a satisfactory life for us requires several kinds of activity which generally cannot be done at the sane time, or at least only partially so. These are work, rest, and play. If you neglect any of these to a serious extent, the others will suffer, It is a false economy to make any one of these your prime occupation and treat the others grudgingly, except under special circumstances and in the short run.

With regard to work, rest, and play, life has three fundamental aspects: physical, social, and spiritual. Each of these requires work, rest, and play. This makes nine basic activities. A human individual must engage in all of these for a full life.

Work, of course, must not be understood in the conventional sense of what you do for money. It is what you do by way of taking care of something. It is what you do as a responsibility.

Physical work may be of many kinds, but it includes the routine care of your body. Some responsibility for keeping the environment tidy also seems appropriate for everyone to share. Other kinds of physical work may consist of more specialized responsibilities.

Physical rest and play are familiar ideas and need no further comment here except to say that although their importance is generally recognized they are too often neglected in practice.

It is a mark of our cultural bias that physical work, rest, and play are recognized as important, whereas the idea of social and spiritual work, rest, and play will seem novel and odd to many.

What I mean by social work is the effort needed to maintain social relationships. Everyone needs, at tines, to go out of his way to maintain friendships and in one way or another to keep the community in good health socially. And, of course, some professionals are devoted to this in whole or in part.

Social rest means leaving one another alone, whether in solitude or in company. Everyone both needs this and needs to do this as a phase of social participation.

Then there is social play, jolly company in its various forms. People think of this as something they do by inclination, but it should also be thought of as an essential part of a satisfying way of life.

Spiritual work is the work of putting your life in order, tending the essential self, contemplating priorities, and making plans. It also includes attending to your education, informing yourself, thinking, cultivating your reason.

Spiritual rest is the kind of meditation where you are not thinking about things, not trying to get things straight, but just letting them sink in. Sleep has this function. So also do reading good novels and poetry, listening to good music, and much of the enjoyment of the arts. Religious rituals may be either spiritual work or spiritual rest or both, depending on their particular characteristics.

Spiritual play is to the mind what physical play is to the body and social play to the social community. It is the exercise of the mind for the sake of the enjoyment of doing so rather than for the sake of the outcome. It includes all sorts of mental games and puzzle solving, as well as the entire realm of comedy. All forms of play have the function of strengthening, limbering up, and improving tone and balance, Physical play does this for the body, social play does it for the social community, and spiritual play does it for the mind.

A lively sense of humor is a universal mark of functional intelligence and balanced values. Good comedy in particular has the characteristic of playfully exploring the boundaries of the acceptable, whether in the realm of basic social values, principles of reason, or conventions of any kind. Through good comedy, whether of the theatrical sort, the exchanging of jokes, anecdotes, and repartee, or games with a comic element, your sense of values is strengthened, kept from becoming rigid and dogmatic, and kept in balance.

When you think of these requirements of a full, life, how poverty-stricken are most lives! No wonder there is so much irritation, so much boredom, so much wasted effort, so much squalor, and so much that is grotesque!

The mixture of these elements will vary from one individual to another, of course. Moreover, just as there are times for going hungry because something else is urgent, so any of these elements may be neglected for the sake of something more important at the time. However, not indefinitely, unless your life is destined to end soon. Self-sacrifice in the form of the neglect of basic needs is self-defeating in the end. It is a case of not caring for your equipment. Only in circumstances of the most desperate urgency is that kind of self-sacrifice consistent with its purpose.

The principle you that should guide you is clear. Only by making cooperative individuality your exclusive basic life policy can you achieve the fullest, most joyful life available to you. The question is how to implement that policy. We do not live in a utopia of our own imagining. In the real world the only fully attainable ideal is your basic life policy. There is nothing to hinder you there other than your own unsteadiness of mind. But with regard to the nine elements of a full life many compromises may be needed. The thing to keep in mind is that the compromises should be made in such a way as to *serve*, never to compromise, the basic policy of cooperative individuality.

Getting your priorities in order is part of your spiritual work. It is not something you can wrap up in a big package once and for all. It is a matter for ongoing management. You need your major commitments in order, but even these should stand the test of ongoing reappraisal. Many of the less major policies, such as your daily habits, may be due for periodic revision as conditions change. And many things have to be decided on the spot. You cannot prescribe your whole life in advance. It is your major priorities, together with the kind of skill we call sensitivity and good judgment, that enable you to act wisely. Sensitivity and good judgment are skills of applying your major priorities in the circumstances of the moment. The development of these skills is also part of your spiritual work.

Reflect now on the implications of cooperative individuality. It seeks the common benefit. What is the common benefit? Would it not be strange if the common benefit were dull and depressing? The common benefit must surely be satisfying on all levels. It must include the peace that only a good conscience can bring. It must include confidence in the helpfulness of others at need. It must include good cheer and playfulness. It must include occasions of celebration. It must include respect for the reality in which we live, respect for our own nature, and devotion to the most important things. It must add up to beauty, peace, mirth, and joy.

To be a participant in the pursuit of this common benefit is not to be a dull, obedient, and unimaginative drudge. It is to be an individual sparkling with idiosyncrasy and humor. It is to be strong in your own judgment and resolute in action. It is to be careful in work, adventurous in play, tranquil in rest.

There are as many ways of being this way as there are individuals. It does not mean being some standard kind of individual. It means being that special kind of individual that only you can be. In the simplest terms, it means fully *being*.

15 Consistency and the Social Community

A community is more than just a number of individuals who care about one another and seek the common benefit. It is also a number of individuals who do things together, who collaborate, and whose lives are coordinated in a variety of ways.

This is the social aspect of a community. This is what takes it more than an arrangement of convenience, it is this aspect of a community that is reflected in the words communion and communication. It is this aspect rather than mutual convenience or utility that is of first importance about a community. We need only reflect on the fact that to be an outcast, even if abundantly provided for in all material ways, is the worst of all fates. People (other animals too) can endure starvation, pain, and other hardships, even to death, without profound dissatisfaction if it is part of their participation in the community. But they cannot endure complete ostracism.

This has implications for what it means to follow through on a policy of cooperative individuality. It means that the cooperative aspect of the policy implies not merely doing things for the common benefit, but doing things together. Moreover, this doing things together is not just for the common benefit; it is *part* of the common benefit.

Working together provides a common benefit:

How wrong and foolish, then, are so many of our working conditions, where the scheme of management is to eliminate social values from the job with a view to getting the job done most "efficiently", while the scheme of the workers is to give the minimum while gaining the maximum! Such is the consequence of a policy of exploitation on the one side combined with a policy of getting by on the other. It is profoundly inefficient because it satisfies no one, even though a useful product results.

Cooperation depends on a mutual understanding of what the intentions are. You cannot meet someone for lunch without an agreement on the place and time. You cannot help build a house without an understanding of who is to do what and when.

Moreover, if you are to enter into a cooperative venture, whether of major or minor proportions, you need to have some confidence that the other parties to it can be relied on to do their part.

The social community, then, depends on agreements of many kinds and on the confidence in the reliability of other parties to those agreements.

Confidence that someone else will carry out his part of an agreement may on occasion be founded on verbal assurances. But in the long run it must be based on actual performance.

Cooperative individuality depends on keeping your word:

For these reasons, being consistent with a policy of cooperative individuality requires you to keep your word except when doing so would entail a more serious breach of the policy.

But there is a more direct way in which consistency requires you to keep your word, and drawing it out will reveal the essence of the social community more clearly.

What is inconsistency?:

Suppose we set aside basic life policies for the moment and ask what it means to be consistent with an agreement. Remember the general meaning of consistency:

To be consistent with an intention is to act and think in accordance with it until either you rescind it or it has no further applicability.

It is not inconsistent to change your mind, but it is inconsistent to neglect or violate the intention if you have not changed your mind.

As an example, let us say you have agreed to meet someone for lunch. In the meantime, for some reason, you would rather not go. So you change your mind and just stay at home. To be sure, you have acted unkindly, but have you been inconsistent? On the surface, it would seem you have not, since it is not inconsistent to change your mind. But let us look more deeply into the nature of the intention.

When two people make an agreement, they do not merely form two separate intentions that happen to coincide, It is not merely that you intend to arrive at the restaurant for lunch and your friend happens to intend to arrive there at the same time. There are these two intentions, but to describe the agreement in these terms is to leave out the fact that it is an agreement. It puts it on the same plane as if your friend said, "I'm going to the meeting of the Residents' Association," and you said, "So am I." This is not an agreement, but only a coincidence of intention.

The difference is that an agreement is an intention jointly formed by two or more parties, not two or more separate intentions that happen to coincide. When you make an agreement you are a party to one shared intention. And of course it is the same if you make a promise. In these cases there is an agent of choice over and above the individuals involved, a communal agent of choice consisting of all the parties to the understanding functioning as a unit.

The only way you can consistently avoid following through on an agreement is to obtain the agreement of the other parties to cancel it (assuming it remains applicable to the circumstances). In other words, only the same group -the same community - that made the decision can change its mind about it. To renege unilaterally on an agreement is to make the group act inconsistently. The group acts through its members, and so if you act inconsistently on behalf of the group the group has acted inconsistently through you. However, since it is an act in which the other members had no initiative, the inconsistency is yours, not theirs, as individuals.

Now, making an explicit verbal undertaking is only one way of entering into shared or communal intentions. After all, the principle of the thing does not depend on the superficial fact that words are exchanged. The point is that an understanding is reached whereby one party is going to depend on the other, and they both know this to be so, and their mutual consent to it has been communicated. (The dependence may be mutual, but need not be, as in the case of a simple promise.)

For example, if you see someone trying to lift a heavy box, and you go over and make a move to take one end, with a gesture implying that you mean to be helpful, following which he takes the other end, the two of you have made an agreement to cooperate in lifting the box. For either of you to drop your end voluntarily when you have the box in the air would be inconsistent. In general, the precedent of actual participation in shared activities constitutes, to a degree, an agreement to follow through in those activities. The implication is that the deeper you are involved in shared activities the more delicate it is to withdraw from then consistently.

The operative factor in shared intentions is the existence of a mutual understanding, not the moves that have been made to bring it about. To behave consistently with shared intentions, you must be sensitive to these mutual understandings. This means, among other things, that you should pay attention to what arouses the expectations of others, so as not to blunder into misunderstandings. For after all, the very existence of a community presupposes a background understanding to the effect that certain modes of communication are being depended on. What are they being depended on for? As signals of what intentions on your part, others can count on you to carry out. In other words, a community is a subtle network of shared intentions.

From these observations, we can see that in a social community the individual essential self is not a separate entity but a socially implicated one. Many of your commitments, and probably those with the highest priority, are shared, that is, you have an understanding with others to the effect that they can depend on you to carry out those commitments. Notice, however, that in saying the essential self is partly shared we at-c not at all diminishing its uniqueness. In general, your part in a shared intention is not the same as the part of another party to it. The sharing consists of the mutual understanding and the dependence, not an identity of commitments.

Shared intention is a communal essential self – a culture:

However, over and above your part in a shared intention and the part of each other party to it, is the communal intention that binds all these into one system. This is of special importance in the larger community which anthropologists call a culture. Such a community has its own essential self that defines the culture, and this is an essential self encompassing many individual lives and spanning many generations. Individuals find their place within that essential self, seeing those larger commitments as their opportunity for making their own commitments to them. Of course, the essential self of the culture is not something in addition to the commitments that individuals make to it, but is just the fabric that those interwoven commitments make up. It is only as individuals rise to the occasion that the culture survives.

Just as a community has an essential self that is made up of the interwoven essential selves of its individual members, so it has an agent self made up of the collaboration of individual agents of choice. For although there is no communal agent of choice separate from individual agents of choice, it is nonetheless true that the community can make choices which no single individual can make. For example, no single individual can wage war, but a community can.

The community therefore also has its own agent self. It is obvious enough that the community has its own complex self, the system of externalities that combines the complex selves of its members. In the case of a culture, this is what remains for archaeologists to study. Or rather, a small part of it is what they study.

Cooperative individuality in all its richness:

We can now see the meaning of cooperative individuality in all its richness. It means living uniquely but not alone. It means being literally, not just metaphorically, a part of a larger individuality. It means grasping the opportunity to share in a creative enterprise in which, far from losing your individuality, you will create it in the shared process of creating those many larger individualities, for there are many levels of community. It means being the design, the shuttle, and the thread in a developing fabric in the creation of which your freedom and your security are the same thing. For, your true security can only consist in making your place in that fabric a sure one. Your place is your individuality as a threefold self, and that is your freedom.

The design is your essential self, the shuttle is your agent self, and the thread is your complex self.

Appendix 1: Aspects of Life Policies Based on the Complex Self Not Described in Chapter 11

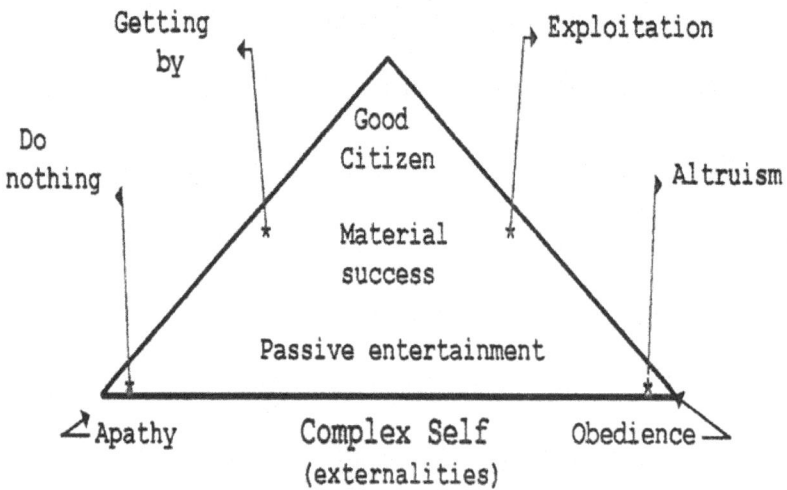

Getting by

Exploitation

Do nothing

Good Citizen

Altruism

Material success

Passive entertainment

Apathy   Complex Self   Obedience
                (externalities)

Getting By - A policy of treating the world as a threatening place in which one must find a niche.

Moving down from the top to the left, the power of choice is still recognized (but off-centre), and commitments are now pretty strongly omitted from the picture. We are now also off-centre on the slope representing externalities, which means that the complex self is not fully accepted. Thus, this policy adds an element of ambivalence. For this policy the colloquial phrase "getting by" is appropriate. Rejecting commitments, grudgingly accepting the power of choice as important but not for its own sake, and only half accepting the complex self, which is seen as the self, this person approaches the world as a basically threatening place in which one must, nonetheless, find a niche for oneself. This may be described as one form of the policy of material success gone sour.

Exploitation – A compulsive policy of acquisition for its own sake.

Looking at the corresponding position to the right of centre, we have the other form of material success gone sour. Here the power of choice is rejected. Commitments are grudgingly accepted as necessary but not for their own sake, and the complex self is only half accepted, though for its own sake. Because of the rejection of the power of choice and the grudging acceptance of commitments, this policy has a certain quality of compulsion about it. Such a policy may be described as "exploitation" - the somewhat compulsive pursuit of externalities but not really in order to enjoy them. The stereotype would be the hard working, money saving, property grabbing individual with a rather miserly attitude.

Apathy – A policy of doing nothing:

This leaves the two policies at the corners of the base. In these positions the ambivalence towards externalities found in getting by and exploitation has become definite rejection, but nothing else is accepted to replace what is rejected. Hence these are policies of dropping out. On the left commitments are totally out of the picture, while only the tail end of the power of choice is recognized. This is an extreme apathy, a policy of doing nothing.

Altruism for short-term profit – A policy of doing superficial favors:

On the right the power of choice is totally out of the picture, while the tail end of commitments is recognized. This therefore is a policy of mere obedience to the supposed beck and call of externalities. Ironically, this is a policy of altruism. The reason for this is that if you are trying to reject the complex self while at the same time basing your policy on it as your conception of the self, you have a conflict that must be resolved so as to have a policy. The easy way to resolve it (and it must be an easy way given the ignoring of the power of choices and the minimal recognition of commitments) is to see your own external interests in the exigencies which arise from the initiatives of others. Consequently, the policy is one of doing favors of an external and usually superficial kind. Such a person is usually thought of as virtuous though somewhat pathetic. But it is not a true virtue, for this kind of altruism is lacking in a true respect for others and utterly lacking in self respect.

Appendix 2: Aspects of Life Policies Based on the Essential Self Not Described in Chapter 11

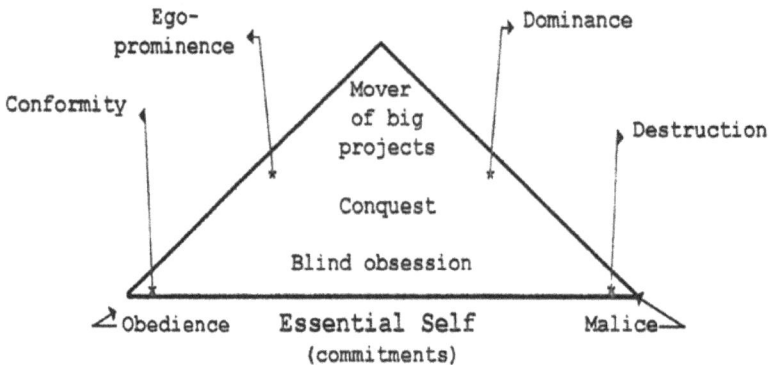

Ego-prominence – A policy pursuing the appearance of being a mover of big deeds:

Moving left halfway down towards the corner, we have largely lost sight of the power of choice but still recognize externalities as important, albeit grudgingly, since they are viewed off-centre. We also have an ambivalent attitude to commitments, being off-centre on this side as well. This person is no longer a single-minded mover of deeds. To resolve the ambivalence about commitments and the grudging acceptance of externalities, this policy replaces the actual moving of deeds with the appearance of doing so. This is therefore the would-be celebrity or "big shot". I call this a policy of ego-prominence.

A little further down towards the corner would be the person on whom such a policy depends for success, the hero-worshipper or celebrity seeker. In a similar way, to the left of blind obsession would be the extreme form of the "true believer', who latches on to someone else's obsession.

Conformity – A policy of mere obedience:

Moving on down to the corner, we have a policy of mere conformity. The power of choice has now been completely lost sight of. Like the altruism just over the ridge, this is a policy of mere obedience, but now it is to the commitments that happen to be available, which are usually the current conventions of the local society.

Petty Martinet – A policy of subduing others to commitments dictated by oneself:

Directly across from ego-prominence, we have a point of view that largely ignores externalities, is ambivalent regarding commitments, and grudgingly accepts the power of choice as important but not as part of the self. Here the combination of recognizing the power of choice while rejecting externalities introduces a sinister quality of sorcery. To resolve the ambivalence, this policy aims at subduing others to commitments dictated by oneself. (A similar resolution is seen in ego-prominence and exploitation.) In its purest form this policy is one of collecting souls (essential selves) as one might collect butterflies. Unlike conquest, it lacks any real devotion to commitments as such. In our society, the concrete stereotype of this policy is not the Devil of fiction but the petty martinet found in many corners of society, whether it be the office manager whose whole concern is with having his orders obeyed, or the bed-ridden granny whose whole concern is to have all those around her running to her beck and call.

Pure Malice – A policy of destruction of essential selves, destruction of all commitments of others:

Moving down to the corner, we again find the ambivalence regarding both commitments and the power of choice giving way to total rejection. Again, since this must be done in the area of commitments, the conflict must be resolved so as to have a policy. The policy will therefore be one of destruction, not destruction in the external arena but destruction of essential selves. Like the diagram itself, this policy tapers down to a policy of pure malice.

Appendix 3: Aspects of Life Policies Based on the Agent Self Not Described in Chapter 11

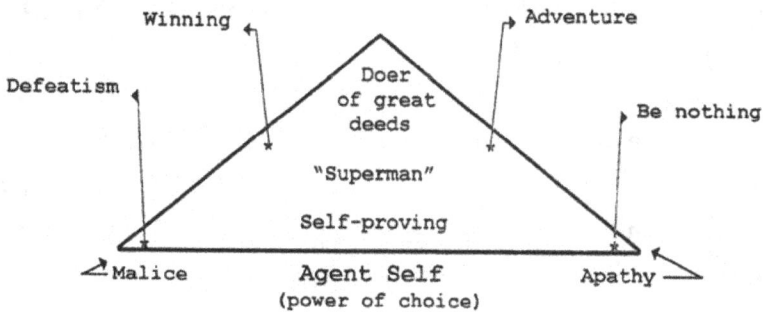

Winning ← ... → Adventure

Defeatism ←

Doer of great deeds

"Superman"

Be nothing →

Self-proving

Malice | Agent Self (power of choice) | Apathy →

Winning – A policy of viewing every occasion as a contest for showing one can do something others can't do:

As we move halfway down towards the left corner, commitments are still recognized as important but externalities are now only slightly considered. The emphasis is still on the power of choice, but we have moved away from centre, so we now have an ambivalent attitude towards it. The easy way to resolve this ambivalence is to set one's own power of choice against others', and so this is a policy of winning. Such a person sees every occasion as presenting a contest in which the idea is to show he can do something the others cannot do.

Defeatism – A policy of malice directed toward one's own essential self:

As we move down to the corner, ambivalence approaches rejection, and so the policy of winning becomes a policy of malice, in this case taking the form of demonstrating the futility of the power of choice. It is a policy of defeatism.

Adventure - A policy of making an entertainment out of exercising choice:

If we move down from the doing of great deeds on the other side, we come to a policy based on the recognition of externalities, though not as belonging to the self, and only a grudging recognition of commitments. Again, we are off-centre on the side of the agent self, and also externalities, so there is ambivalence. Here the easy way to resolve the ambivalence is to drop the idea that it matters what one can do, and the ambivalent attitude to externalities makes this easier, since one can now just make an entertainment out of exercising the power of choice. This is a policy of adventure. The stereotypes are those who attempt to cross the ocean in balloons and other such antics.

As we move down to the corner, again ambivalence becomes rejection. Since commitments are totally ignored, this is another form of apathy, the intention or wish to be nothing.

Editor Comment

In our last two face-to-face talks near the end of Will
Crichton's terminal illness in late 2002, we reminisced about
old Ann Arbor days and friends and families, and of course
philosophy as always. We discussed many things including his
wishes concerning his major work – Foundations for a New
Civilization. Fortunately, almost as an afterthought, I asked
him about publishing a manuscript he had written for use as a
text while teaching adults enrolled in evening philosophy
classes entitled Why Waste Your Life? After a thoughtful
silence he said "I'll leave that up to you."

The manuscript presents an impressive tour de force
of an answer to a central issue in the history of Western
Philosophy – What is the good life? It must have made for a
wonderful experience for his adult students.

My hesitation until now in its publication has been due to
an observation made repeatedly by a wonderful editor of some
of my own work, Louise Waller. She is fond of reminding me
that I will not be there beside the reader to explain what I

mean. Of course Will Crichton was there to explain to his students, which is a major advantage of writing for one's own students. But I had a difficult time thinking that readers could or would want to wade through Why Waste Your Life without his help.

The problem isn't that the original manuscript is so complicated that the reader can't understand it without help. Quite the contrary. Crichton's training as a logician as well as his careful approach to problem solving led him where good mathematicians and logicians go. Take what is a short but complicated question, such as "What is the good life?" and unravel it into an argument made up of simple steps, but much longer. Therefore the reader needs help in keeping it simple as well as staying with the argument to the end of the journey, or at least till an oasis along the way.

After ten years, my courage to edit the manuscript overcame my hesitancy to change a word of Crichton's writing. I don't believe the result has changed any of the ideas he presented. Purposefully, no changes were made to clarify or "correct" his work even where my personal view differs from his conclusions or there seems to be ambiguity. Changes were made in an effort to help tell the reader what Crichton means without him being there. Mostly this meant changing the organization in such a way that his ideas were placed in context of related ideas. And of course, an attempt was made to correct obvious typographical errors, a seemingly never ending job in all publication. Construction of a detailed table of contents and addition of the appendices were part of the attempt to make the book easier to navigate.

ABOUT THE AUTHOR

Will Crichton was Professor in the Faculty of Philosophy at
The University of Toronto teaching philosophy for many years.
He authored *Foundations for a New Civilization* and co-
authored a translation of Rilke's *The Duino Elegies*. He
received his PhD in philosophy from The University of
Michigan. Born August 30, 1928 in Toronto, he died December
5, 2002 in Toronto.

www.ingramcontent.com/pod-product-compliance
Lightning Source LLC
Chambersburg PA
CBHW050353280326
41933CB00010BA/1443